The Qualitative
Elementary
School

Exploration Series in Education

Under the Advisory Editorship of John Guy Fowlkes

The Qualitative Elementary School

CHARACTERISTICS OF AN EXCELLENT CURRICULUM

Duane Manning

Professor of Education, Arizona State University

Harper & Row, Publishers
New York, Evanston, and London

To Mother
who was my first and finest teacher,
and to David
for whom I wish a better world.

THE QUALITATIVE ELEMENTARY SCHOOL
CHARACTERISTICS OF AN EXCELLENT CURRICULUM

I-O
Library of Congress Catalog Card Number: 63–11295

Contents

Editor's Introduction

Since the appearance of *Why Johnny Can't Read,* in 1955, numerous treatises on various aspects of the educational program in the United States have appeared. Some of these works have been directed at specific subject matter areas such as the one previously mentioned, while others have been sweeping denunciations of some level of education, namely, elementary schools, secondary schools, the undergraduate college program, or indeed the program of graduate education.

In recent months the term "quality" has been considered in relation to educational institutions, particularly on the secondary and collegiate levels. The work presented here analyzes this concept of quality in the elementary school. A perusal of the table of contents reveals that not only are the three R's given serious attention, but so are two large S's along with creativity, discipline and supportive design.

This is a well-written volume, challenging, evaluative and suggestive. One reader of this work commented: "flashes of brilliance are found in this writing."

In light of the above characteristics of this book, it is clear that this work is both timely and usable. It should be of marked assistance to all those concerned with the education of elementary school children.

JOHN GUY FOWLKES

January, 1963

vii

Preface

This book is devoted to an interpretation of excellence in the elementary school. Presumably, in the thousands of books written about elementary curriculum and methods there is much that is inconsequential. What kinds of practices might more appropriately be stressed if our schools wish to increase significantly their effectiveness? This book suggests an answer to that question. Using a traditional organization that is familiar to most of the schools, it attempts to pull from this framework some of the larger and more dynamic ideas. Each idea is referred to as a qualitative factor. Eighty-three such factors are identified.

It would be unwarranted, of course, to claim that these factors are the most qualitative that can be proposed. No one could authoritatively make such a claim any more than he could authoritatively claim that they are not. The ideas that have been interpreted simply project one image of a qualitative school. They reflect the kind of a school I would like my own son to attend. Each idea has been carefully selected, however, because of a special contribution which it can make to the total program. In their entirety, therefore, they constitute a considerable array of strength.

Each period of time seems to present its own special obstacles to the achievement of excellence in the schools. Many of the obstacles today relate to splinter movements and oversimplification of the task. Some for instance wish to go back to the little red schoolhouse although the color now appears to have been wrong, the heating and plumbing were bad, and the ability range was almost intolerable. Others speak blandly of the "beefed up" curriculum. This conveys the image of an overfed steer. Such a creature thrives well in a protected environment, but in a world of conflict for survival it is no match for a predatory bear. Perhaps it would be safer to design a curriculum with more of the characteristics of a tiger.

Excellence is a many-splendored thing and must be sought through a more balanced and comprehensive approach. The concentration of ideas presented here should help the reader to see a larger sweep of the learning environment, and to increase his understanding of what is involved. I hope that the interpretation will be able to convey something of the spirit of excellence as well as its strength, and that it will reflect a quality of the heart as well as the mind. Perhaps the description will be interesting and provocative even if it falls short of the image of quality we shall eventually conceive.

DUANE MANNING

Tempe, Arizona

The Qualitative
Elementary
School

Chapter 1

Qualitative Schools

The public image of a qualitative school is fascinating in itself. The teacher in such a school would speak the language of the philosopher and the physicist. He would at the same time, however, reflect the best qualities of Horatio at the Bridge, Davy Crockett at the Alamo, and Daniel Boone in "Old Kaintuck'." He would be so sensitively attuned to the inner thoughts and feelings of children that he would be constantly aware of their psychic vibrations. Simultaneously, however, he would be hardy enough to endure withering criticism.

The building, too, would be a phenomenal creation and would be subject to similar stress and contradiction. It would remain a janitor's delight in the sense that he could simply hose it down, and it would continue to bear nobly its characteristic motifs of indestructibility and antisepsis. Yet, it would be aesthetically exciting like a scoop of the sky and grace the campus like the Taj Mahal.

In the days to come perhaps the schools may assume what some regard as a more scientific posture and develop cluster curriculums that derive from more concentrated and pervasive intents. Thus, a parent might choose for his child a school that clustered its program around a central purpose—such as academic achievement, life adjustment, or personality development—and he could make his choice from these more clearly defined areas of emphasis. This might eliminate some of the difficulties inherent in making the school all things to all people, for the differences in point of view are admittedly great and creating schools that do justice to all is relatively impossible.

Yet, in the meantime, that is precisely what has to be done. The schools are not clustered by basic intent and they are not likely to be. They exist in a multivalue setting serving a heterogeneous and discriminating clientele. For the foreseeable future they will continue to carry the special burdens as well as the special strengths of a multipurpose role. What then is a qualitative school?

The point of view to be reflected here is that a qualitative school in such a setting must by necessity be a blend. This is not to be regarded as either fortunate or unfortunate, but merely as one of the conditions accepted for the discussion. The blending together of hope and reality is after all a process that one exercises throughout his life. He would like to build a $50,000 home but builds instead a home which he can afford. He would like to own a luxurious automobile designed in the tradition of continental elegance, but may buy instead a car that looks as though it had been built under a rug. He would like a mate generously endowed with intelligence, beauty, personality, and character but somewhere along the way has adjusted his expectations. The qualitative school as interpreted here will be a blend, but hopes to be an exciting and excellent one nonetheless.

The six characteristics which follow constitute a particular concept or image of the qualitative school. They amount to an interpretation of quality rather than a definition. Each of them is a general or pervading sort of characteristic, and collectively they reflect a setting in which the more specific factors that are to be developed later can properly function.

Goal-Directed Activity

Over in Lexington where the first blows were struck for freedom a Harvard team has carefully guided some experimentation with team teaching. The team teaching concept shatters the present insulation of the teacher and creates a diffusion of effort.

Up in Bay City, Michigan, an administration concerned with the amount of trivia that is imposed upon teachers with its consequent loss of precious time, has developed a thoughtful procedure for preserving more teaching time for more significant teaching tasks.

Down in the midwest Champaign has made a major study of phonics, Indiana has pioneered in an economical approach to educational television, and Appleton has refined its grip on the non-graded school.

Throughout the nation individual schools have reached out to test, study, and refine their programs. Some of the efforts may not prove to be beneficial, but it is beneficial to make the try. Innovation or experimentation is one of the marks of a healthy school organism.

Just as a society is able to develop a culture when it is sufficiently stable and organized to have leisure time and a leisure class, so can the school when it is stable and well organized find the time and resources to hypothesize about and refine its program. If the school is qualitative, it is probably doing things—trying some new ways, blazing some new trails, forging ahead on one or more fronts. It always has the door open to creative suggestions from its faculty and community. This is a characteristic possessed in common by the best schools in the nation. A school can be up and doing without being qualitative, but it can't be qualitative unless it is up and doing. The best schools are carrying on some kind of major goal-directed activity.

Multiple Offense

The qualitative school brings into play a selective and powerful array of ideas. It has both reach and depth. Like a successful modern coach it has a versatile offense. It may know seven or eight qualitative ingredients that should be a conscious part of its grouping practices. It may know an equal number of qualitative ingredients that make up an excellent system of reporting to parents. It knows a number of ways to maximize the effectiveness of scheduling the day's activities. It knows, regardless of the pattern of organization which it adopts, the qualitative organizational factors that should find expression.

In addition to this powerful range of many ideas about how to get a job done, it possesses also a significant understanding of selectivity. It knows for instance of a single idea in spelling which may at one stroke pay a 95 percent dividend. It knows because of its acquaintance with the research on handwriting how the improvement of only four letters of the alphabet may often contribute a 45 percent improvement in legibility. It knows which factor in the reading program is protein and which is dessert, and it knows the approaches to mathematics that can produce more understanding and less memorization.

It is a school with sufficient resources in ideas that when one thing doesn't work it simply tries another. It is sufficiently informed that it has a grasp of possible qualitative factors throughout the entire learning environment. It, therefore, has the wherewithal to push ideas through to completion.

Demonstrated Results

The qualitative school will get a job done and will be able to show results. Its children will learn to read independently and with meaning. They will handle rudimentary mathematical processes with more understanding than most of their parents. They will have an intellectual curiosity and skill in scientific enquiry that will take your breath away. They will know more about the geography and history of their country than most adults, and more importantly, they will see it as a series of interrelated factors. They will show the effects of a healthy and effective discipline where permissiveness and restraints exist in a proper and balanced relationship. They will mix work and play in the right proportions and rhythm so that each is reinforced by the other. The school, in short, will turn out children at the end of the sixth grade who are informed, skilled, well-behaved young citizens eager for the next lap of the journey. Their curiosity is whetted, their mental health is strengthened, and they are capable of moving with considerably more independence through the junior high school years.

If an elementary school cannot do this in six or seven years with most of its youngsters, it is probably not a qualitative school.

A Continuing Concern for Children

The qualitative school has never abandoned its deep and abiding concern for each child in its custody. It is not shaken by the fact that loud and powerful voices ridicule the concept of the whole child for it knows this is precisely what comes to school. It does not angrily denounce the voices, for many are sincere; but it recognizes them as being more loud than informed and more emotional than wise in the ways of children. So rather than retreat from its attempt to give each child an enlightened and humanistic education it becomes more resolute in its determination to do so.

This concern for children means many things. It means identifying and developing their unique qualities. It means being responsive to their feelings and aspirations, their strengths and weaknesses. And it means helping them to find in the curriculum a place where they can be comfortable and successful and secure.

In an unbalanced or exaggerated emphasis, the child development factor can lead to some fundamental errors. It can lead to unbridled permissiveness and glorification of I-ness or individuality over We-ness or group endeavor. This is more hurtful than helpful. The child's individuality is a precious thing, but it must find outlet and expression in a society characterized by groups. The same basic concern which causes one to respect and value individuality requires sensitivity and respect for the feelings and individuality of others as well. The qualitative school doesn't make this error. It isn't like a parent who pampers and spoils his children. It is more like the parent who loves and respects them, but holds them accountable.

No school will be qualitative without such a concern. No school with a claim to leadership will retreat. It will stand up tall to be counted on this issue. It will say to all who wish to hear:

This child is a precious thing. Try to know him well. Bring him into your classroom as a loved and esteemed member of the group. Respect him for what he is. Help him to discover and develop the things that he can do best. Help him grow in wisdom and in skill. Teach him that he has within him a capacity for greatness. Give him the will to touch the stars. Protect him and cherish him and help him to become his finest self.

A Continuing Concern for Our Way of Life

Along with an unmistakable concern for children the qualitative school shows an unmistakable concern for our way of life. It teaches the traditions and cherishes the spirit that made this a great and kindly nation. It tries intelligently to reflect this way of life in the fundamental operations of the school by giving children a voice, letting them experience citizenship at increasing levels of maturity, and helping them to achieve as they go through school a growing independence of thought and action that is the hallmark of a free and powerful people.

As a mirror of democracy it will not tolerate arbitrary and unreasonable behavior from its administration and faculty simply because they are adults. It will not stand for any form of physical or mental brutality in its classroom. It will not allow a child to be hurt or to receive an inferior education because of the pigment in his skin. For it is an instrument of society, guided by a basic respect for human dignity, seeking to reflect and perpetuate all that is best in our way of life.

It opens its doors, it opens its mind, it opens its heart, and it says proudly:

Take all of these children—Catholic and Jew, Negro and white, ragged and rich, handicapped and gifted . . . and teach them to respect and appreciate one another. Help them look beyond their individual needs to consider the common good. Help them preserve their individualities, but to grow in their ability to enrich the quality of group living. Teach them that men are brothers, and help them develop a sensitivity to the problems and aspirations of others. Teach them a love for our way of life, and help them understand their role in a way of living which can elevate all mankind.

A Flexible and Enlightened Administration

And last, the qualitative elementary school demonstrates a flexible and enlightened administration that seeks creatively to implement the curriculum rather than to restrain it. It is an administration which properly regards itself as a servant rather than a master, as an arm of the total enterprise rather than a judge advocate. In too many schools the administration still suffers from inflated ego and impoverished insight.

One imaginative teacher teaches in a school where the administrator told her not to bring pets to school for it would upset the children. Another teaches in a school where she was asked not to take a field trip for it would upset the community. A fourth grade teacher with bright children was told not to move into fifth grade material because it would upset the next teacher. No wonder some schools are in difficulty!

There are some communities where unsuccessful high school

coaches have been removed from their jobs and placed in the principalship of an elementary school! There are many graduate schools where men frustrated in their basic vocational choice are preparing for the elementary school principalship. Such factors tragically weaken the school. The principal should be a leader. His personal qualities of leadership should exist *in addition to his intimate understanding of the elementary school.* He can be a leader because of this understanding. How can anyone be a leader of an enterprise which he does not understand?

The qualitative elementary school will not exist without a flexible and enlightened administration. Like an All-American quarterback it knows when to run for a touchdown and when to tighten its defenses. Like a skillful expediter it knows how to circumvent and resolve the trifling obstacles that constantly stand in the way of innovation. Like a brilliant wartime commander it knows how to hedgehop the many unimportant islands of activity and move in on the target. Without such masterminding the resources of the school mill around at cross purposes and never become coordinated at an effective level. This is no job for a boy scout, or a do-gooder, or an unsuccessful high school coach, or a "friend" of the school board. It's a job for the most qualified persons the district has in its elementary schools, those who are eminently successful in their relations with children and colleagues, those who know their jobs inside and out.

Such persons are worth all the community can pay them. Their salary could properly be equivalent to that of a United States Senator, but there isn't a single community in the United States that has had the perspicacity to recognize this. When and if communities do wake up to this matter, they may substantially increase the incidence of that healthy breed of emerging young administrator who moves out of his office into the classroom helping to plan and expedite the ideas of a creative faculty and community.

Summary

And so the qualitative elementary school is interpreted for the purpose of this discussion. It is a school that proudly continues to show a deep and abiding concern for children. It is a school which knows and employs a powerful and versatile array of techniques to help each child become the most that he may become. Assisted by a flexible and enlightened administration, it gets a job done giving children in six or seven years of elementary schooling a big boost forward in all areas of the curriculum. And it leaves children with a healthy feeling of love and respect for our way of life. This is the image of quality to be projected in the succeeding chapters of this book.

Chapter 2

Social Studies in the Elementary School

There are some who feel today that social studies as an area of the curriculum is caught in a squeeze. It does not, like reading, belong to the Power Block. It is not a Glamour Boy like science. It has never achieved the Respectability of mathematics. And it is not a Fair-haired Child like the languages. What, then, can one say it is?

In the most common and traditional sense, social studies consists of geography, history, and civics. In a diffused and larger sense, however, social studies is every day in the school, every child in the classroom, and every personal relationship that occurs in the program. It is helping every child to hold his head high and to know that he is a worthy person. It is extending wider the ripples of understanding that indicate a growing awareness of one's world. It is kindness and love, tolerance and ideals, sacrifice and maturity. It is a massive story about man, about his problems, his aspirations, his way of life, and how he fits into the mainstream of the world's culture.

It would be difficult to conceive of a part of the curriculum that has greater potential or importance than social studies. For, if history is the story of man, what area of the curriculum has a more exciting and revealing story to tell? If social studies can help to enlighten man about the world in which he lives, when in all recorded history has he needed more to be truly enlightened? And if today man has a special need to be able to peer into the future for a glimpse of what tomorrow may bring, from what better torch can he be guided than the thoughtful illumination of what has already occurred?

The inclination in some schools today to whittle down the social studies in order to direct more time and emphasis to other aspects of the curriculum is shortsighted and can result only in a qualitative loss. Social studies, instead, should be reaffirmed and reemphasized. The following factors are submitted as being characteristic of an excellent program.

The Classroom as a Laboratory for Social Living

It is possible that the richest and most dynamic source of content available to social studies is largely unworked and perhaps unrecognized. Good schools may build up their stores of enrichment materials in the form of excellent books and materials. They may even build them carefully in terms of field experiences and environmental resources. Simultaneously, however, they may fail to identify the classroom living itself as a vital source of content in their program. This source of content is richer than anything that can be found in a book, and lies always at the disposal of the thoughtful teacher. It is unparalleled in the degree to which it is meaningful to the learners, and it has its own built-in or intrinsic motivation.

Hardly a day goes by in the classroom without some sort of misbehavior or interpersonal stress on the part of the students. A child may strike another child; he may lie about, deprive, or otherwise malign a classmate. Such conditions are widely regarded by teachers as difficult or unpleasant. But is it not possible at the same time to recognize that these negative situations afford in themselves a unique opportunity for improving the classroom living? The fact that such an incident takes place in the presence of the class gives the members sufficient understanding of it to form a basis for resolving it. And the act of resolving it is the process of improving one's own social living.

The other side of the coin is equally rich and important. The classroom is also the stage for virtuous acts on the part of one or more of the children. Alfred successfully mediates and stops a fight. Linda defends an unpopular view in the class discussion and calmly presents an overlooked aspect of justice. The class demonstrates suspended judgment in the face of circumstantial evidence and refuses to make a decision until it has more complete facts. The children show in their selection of class officers that they can look beyond the superficial aspects of personality and social status and recognize leadership. In every school there are positive elements of social living that deserve recognition; and the process of thoughtful recognition is a positive contribution to improving the quality of social living. It must be done carefully. It must not play on over-emotionalism or oversentimentalism. It is probably best done with modesty and restraint; but it is important that it be done. The use of actual classroom events for such purposes is a qualitative element of the first order of importance.

The logical extension of this concept is to use the school and its environs as a laboratory for social education. The qualitative social studies program will selectively extract the richest opportunities it may have to help children experience social education in a realistic and guided setting. The accumulation of these experiences throughout the elementary years helps a child to be more understanding and informed about life. It helps to season him and quicken his grasp of the important link between freedom and responsibility. It provides him with opportunity and encouragement to become a finer person by being a contributing part of something larger than himself. The qualitative program will make such learnings a conscious part of its day by day operations.

Developing Ideals

There are those who believe that schools should no longer attempt to contribute to the development of ideals and that this is a function which should be more appropriately left to the church and the home. It is possible to build a rather strong case for this point of view and to arrive at the decision with complete sincerity. Such a decision, of course, rests with the parents, for they are the final arbiters. The position taken here, however, is that the development of ideals is an essential function of the school in general and the social studies in particular. To leave it out of the program is a tragic omission and a vast waste of opportunity, for the curriculum affords many advantageous moments that are not so easily available to either the church or the home.

After the reported incidents of rigged quiz shows an American history teacher in New Jersey taught his class an important lesson. A majority of his students seemed to feel that it was all right for quiz contestants to have accepted answers, and he was deeply concerned about their attitude. So he made up a quiz on American history and hinted to nine of his students that he wouldn't mind if they looked at the answers lying on his desk. They did and got perfect scores. The remaining members of the class flunked. Then the teacher revealed what he had done. All the members who had flunked the test objected violently and complained about the unfairness of the situation. "All right," he told them, "we will now have another discussion of rigged T.V. shows."

Perhaps most teachers would have argued with the students in an attempt to differentiate for them between right and wrong. This man was more imaginative and inspired. He taught them a lesson they are not likely to forget.

History abounds in instances of courage, fortitude, perserverance, vision, honesty, and their negative counterparts. From what better source can a nation find opportunity to present to youth its national conscience and ideals?

In the past the awareness of ideals has been occasionally stressed through the study of great men. Some teachers include such an emphasis throughout the year employing a project called "The Hall of Fame." The Hall of Fame may be symbolized by a special place set aside in the room, an appropriate picture, or a three dimensional construction. As great men come to the attention of the class in its study of history, science, or the arts, they receive appropriate emphasis. Any child in the room may decide that one of these great men merits being in the Hall of Fame. He then studies the life of the person and attempts to prepare a stimulating and persuasive presentation which he gives to the class in the form of a nomination. The class itself decides who will be honored by being placed in its Hall of Fame. Such an approach has a continuity of focus on greatness. In the hands of a sensitive and skillful teacher it can have a powerful impact.

In recent times the great man approach has received a special sort of criticism. It has been accused of misleading young people by giving them an exaggerated and perhaps even false picture of the virtues of some of the great figures of the past. Some of this criticism may be valid. One should never make a dishonest portrayal. Human frailty and limitations can be a part of such study, and the approach can be a genuine searching process in which lack of vision and errors in judgment may take their place in the unfolding of a great man's life. This does not cheapen the man to children. In fact it may endear him more and make his greatness seem more plausible. The approach today can be perhaps less of the concept of great men and more of the concept of greatness in men. This approach seems qualitative both in conception and in results.

The Selective Core of Information

Professional education in modern times has not generally placed a very high value on information itself. The gross national product of Brazil, the number of inches of rainfall in Ecuador, the problem of erosion in Mesopotamia have not been regarded as extremely vital matters to young children. This is understandable and is in part a reaction against an earlier emphasis on hosts of unrelated and miscellaneous trivia. Also, it is probably true that it is impossible to identify a core of information that is equally important for all children to learn. Presumably, however, there is a body of information falling within the special province of the social studies which is relatively desirable for most children to know even if one cannot prove that such information is absolutely essential.

For instance, it is desirable after six years in the elementary school for a child to be informed about the early settlement of his country, the westward movement, and the development of the United States as a nation. It is desirable that he be informed about the great men and women who have played major roles in the nation's growth, about great moments or events that were crucial in the process, and about the motivations and circumstances that blended together to mold the eventual results. There should be a discernible core of information in the social studies program which is defensible in terms of criteria of content that are consciously applied.

One such criterion might be simply that this is a type of information children in America should know. For example, they should know about the Mayflower, The Boston Tea Party, and the Constitutional Convention.

Another criterion might have to do with types of information that are desirable or necessary as a groundwork for later steps in the sequence. The first grader who works with crude neighborhood maps and experiences their meaning and purpose is in a better state of readiness to understand grid systems and eventually the products of the cartographer. The child who is guided in his social perceptions through an understanding of his own expanding neighborhood may be in a better position to grapple with the concept of the expanding world community.

A third criterion might logically focus upon the local environment. Because of the variation in communities a given school should selectively build up an inventory of information that it especially wishes its own children to know. The community may have its special hazards, problems, accomplishments, strengths, or a special place in history. Such information should be inventoried and stressed.

The point is simply that schools could, by giving their best judgment to the matter, ascertain a much more selective and valuable nucleus of information than is currently being taught. The information could then be accorded a higher priority in the program. This process of selective identification is a team job. It requires the assistance of the subject matter specialist and is best accomplished when the interested parties gather and think collectively about what is important for children to know. It is admittedly a time consuming process; but almost everything that is really worth doing is time consuming. Even if one never achieved the degree of refinement desired he at least brings about a more select core of information than he had at the beginning of his quest. His content is therefore qualitatively improved.

There is one additional ramification of this that seems worth noting. Social studies has commonly been regarded as the core of the elementary program. In this capacity content and experiences in social studies make an important contribution to the other areas of the curriculum. For instance, the social studies and language arts are interwoven with mutual benefit to each, for language arts has no content of its own and social studies without language is inarticulate. Creativity, also, may receive impetus and a point of departure from the substance of social studies. One can paint Lincoln and capture the greatness of his spirit because he knows the greatness of the man. One can project in his creativity more imagination and color, perhaps because his mind is splashed with color from the great moments of his nation's past. No area of the curriculum is independent of the social studies. In varying degrees it serves a contributing or feeder relationship to them all. It will serve this feeder relationship on a higher level of excellence as its content is more selectively derived.

Critical Thinking

Some of the schools today are helping children develop an understanding and skill in what is frequently called critical thinking. Critical thinking is misnamed and is not so much critical as it is adequate. It means helping a child to look on both sides of a matter, as well as at the top and the bottom, and square in the middle. Most adults, of course, have not learned to do this. This more objective approach to life is similar to the motivation of the philosopher who seeks to achieve total understanding of total reality. Human frailty is such that the philosopher may privately concede his task is futile, but he does not abandon the quest. In a sense, the social studies program is a setting for the development of the young philosopher, nourishing in him the desire to exercise increasing intelligence in living.

This is heady wine. One is tampering here with the stuff of maturity. If this can be developed in children, the school has given them a skill which can be used throughout their entire span of life. It could help them to be less naïve and shortsighted than the generations which have preceded them. It could help equip them to meet the uncertain nature of tomorrow more resourcefully, and to toughen their minds for the problems which somehow seem destined to grow more difficult as the future unfolds. How do schools come to grips with this?

Each of the qualitative factors suggested up to this point have some relationship or contribution to make to critical thinking. Use of the classroom as a laboratory for social living nourishes it daily, and use of the school and its environs as a laboratory for social education gives it greater perspective and realism. The selective core of information provides better ammunition for thinking. Helping children to develop ideals provides the essential ingredients of values and sense of direction. Even the feeder function points up the criss-cross nature of relationships that are a vital part of thinking. From each of these one thoughtfully extracts the elements that will assist children to bring intelligence to bear on their living; but the school can do more than this to develop it.

One practice that is yielding good results is the preplanned free-wheeling type of discussion during which the class goes to work on a topic the children themselves want to talk about. Generally, a rotating panel of children solicits possible choices of topics from the individual members of the class, and the decision as to the topic is made a day or so before the discussion is to be held. During the discussion, the teacher moves to the side lines and allows it to become a child-directed experience. He may move into the discussion briefly only when needed, but makes a deliberate effort to stay out as much as possible. Under such circumstances children may be expected to make some surprising choices of topics. One sixth grade class chose the topic "Should sixth graders go steady?" A traditionalist might not permit such a matter to be discussed in his classroom. This particular teacher felt that it served a useful purpose to allow children to get it out in the open, and that the children's *choice* of topics as well as what they had to say about them was extremely valuable in helping him to have a better understanding of his students.

Over and above the values mentioned, the free-wheeling discussion provides a setting for critical thinking. One thinks better when one is informed; but being informed is not enough. The information and ideas one holds need to be placed in a setting or context in which they may be challenged, and in which the essential sifting, weighing, comparing, testing and reappraising of cherished beliefs may take place. Recording and playing back the discussion may provide an additional powerful learning opportunity.

Another aspect of critical thinking which is largely untested involves teaching children to recognize and understand the standard propaganda devices; name calling, the glittering generality, transfer, testimonial, plain folks, band wagon, and card stacking are within the comprehension of many elementary children. The current events program is a fertile medium for this teaching, but much of the class study and discussion may be involved. There is little doubt that children can learn such devices, but there is reasonable doubt that some parents and teachers can stand up under it after they have been taught. The average adult has a lot of growing of his own to do in this regard, and placing these tools within the understanding of children may painfully accelerate the process.

All areas of the curriculum have some responsibility for nourishing critical thinking, but social studies because of its meaning and pervasive nature has a special responsibility in this regard. The qualitative program deliberately involves learners in situations where they are encouraged to think, it shows respect for their ideas, and it seeks constantly to raise the level at which they can function. There is no substitute for this factor and few human achievements enjoy a higher claim to priority.

The Self-Direction Function

A study made in Indiana came up with some interesting and significant results. This study attempted to determine how much self-direction was evident in classes in social studies ranging from the second to twelfth grades.[1]

Data for the study was obtained by observing the classes in action. The observation focused on twelve criteria which were designed in such a way that all happenings, events, and circumstances taking place in the social studies period might be classified with respect to being teacher-directed or pupil-directed.

The findings indicated that in each of the twelve situations studied the predominant emphasis was as one might suspect, teacher-directed. The least teacher-directed situation was directive in the ratio of 4 to 1. The most highly teacher-directed situation was directive in the ratio of 90 to 1. The overall emphasis was directive to the extent of 14 to 1. Not a single observation in the entire study turned out to be self-directive even though one of the two schools selected for the observations was a laboratory school which was purportedly permissive and pupil-centered in its approach.

Perhaps the finding which was of greatest significance to this discussion was the one indicating that the amount of directiveness reflected in the classrooms tended to increase at advancing grade levels. That is to say, that with younger children who are presum-

[1] Duane Manning, "An Analysis of the Relative Directiveness of Instruction," *Studies in Education,* Bulletin no. 2 (1950), Indiana University Press, pp. 81–85.

ably less mature and less capable of assuming any large degree of direction of their own class living, there was more evidence of self-direction than with older children who are presumably more mature and more capable of assuming that function. This is a most provocative finding and merits careful reflection. How can a free society which prizes self-direction as an indispensable aspect of its way of life condone an approach which tends to restrict or deny experiences in self-direction?

The position taken here is that schools should provide and encourage experiences in self-direction at successively higher levels of responsibility and maturity. Furthermore, such experiences are specifically and logically a function of the social studies. A classroom that moves along day by day without even providing "spot situations" in which pupils are allowed to try their wings and manage their own affairs is denying children an important avenue to growth and maturity. A classroom that seeks conscientiously to provide expanding experiences in pupil-planning and self-management is demonstrating a higher conception of its role and is making a finer contribution to a democratic way of life. The social studies program which is most qualitative will press forward vigorously on this front.

Teaching for Depth

One of the great strengths of social studies is the wealth of content from which it may draw. The entire range of social sciences lies at its disposal and it may legitimately select whatever it may need from the fields of sociology, psychology, and anthropology as well as from geography and history. This tremendous latitude poses a special vulnerability and frequently results in a scattered and superficial program. Thus, social studies has been aptly compared to the Powder River in Montana—"a mile wide and a foot deep." How can the program achieve greater depth?

The more selective core of information will make a contribution to resolving the problem particularly with reference to the gradative nature of sequential experiences that are planned for the total elementary program. This is not ordinarily done well in the elementary school. There is an old story about the father who went to school to complain about his child's units. He told the teacher that in kindergarten the boy had studied boats, and in the first and second grades he again studied boats. Now he was in the third grade and they were still studying boats! Why couldn't they get his child off a boat and on to a train? The story contains more truth than humor. The modern programs have not been well engineered in this regard and children have studied some of the same units year after year. This has been particularly true of units on Indians, and the theme of community helpers is sometimes taught in the kindergarten as well as in the first and second grades. This is too much of a good thing. There are too many matters of major importance in social studies to justify such units being taught over and over again at different grade levels. The present six-year program of study might easily be taught in four years.

One of the significant efforts to get more depth in the program is to identify more carefully the total thrust of the program and to carve out the major contributions that can be made at each grade level. Suppose, for instance, that a given school decided to limit the preplanned portion of its program to twenty-four major units which would be assigned in the proportion of four units to each grade. Naturally, these units would be carefully chosen to reflect the best cross section and richest kind of learning experiences that could be proposed. Inasmuch as twenty-four is less than half the number ordinarily taught, there is opportunity to study each unit more carefully. What is basically involved is the thoughtful pursuit of a smaller number of units selectively chosen for each grade level.

This idea is well interpreted by Preston, who recommends use of the type-study unit in categories such as the following:

1. A minority culture such as Negro or Navaho.
2. A neighboring culture such as Canada or Mexico.
3. An unknown, remote culture such as China or India.
4. A stable democratic culture such as Switzerland or Denmark.
5. An isolated society such as Australia or Andorra.[2]

Preston's idea contains a good one-two punch. It would focus study on a unit that was an excellent example of the category it was to represent and would involve a careful exploration of that

[2] Ralph C. Preston, *Teaching Social Studies in the Elementary School,* New York, Holt, Rinehart & Winston, 1958, p. 160.

particular culture. Then it would follow through with comparisons and generalizations concerning similar types of cultures. The idea is to achieve depth, and subsequent activity is directed at establishing those intelligent relationships and associations that are the mark of the well-educated person.

A second emerging practice involves the use of single topic books. A social studies text normally covers a great deal of ground, and for reasons of brevity does so in a rather sketchy manner. One of the more recent publications begins with Leif the Lucky and ends with the United Nations organization. It contains twenty-six chapters, each one encompassing an era and averaging about eighteen pages per era. The child can get a good overall view in such a presentation; but if he attempts to pursue a given era in depth he will not get much satisfaction from similar texts. Textbooks, in general, are extremely poor reference works. The child requires single topic books in order to pursue his subjects, and these are now available in rapidly increasing number from sources other than the textbook publishers. These books are called trade books because they are sold in bookstores to the general public. They are often stimulating and authentic, and are a necessary adjunct to the school that seeks greater depth in its program.

There is a third aspect of depth which may be appropriate to mention at this point. It has to do with the teacher and his depth in scholarship with respect to the total teaching task. Obviously, the elementary teacher cannot be a specialist in each of the subjects he must teach unless team teaching or departmentalization methods are used. These methods provide basic subject competence, but do so at a professional price that many elementary schools do not choose to pay. The delimiting of the number of units to be taught at any given grade may open up another way. Although the elementary teacher may not be a specialist in social studies, he can achieve a degree of specialization in those portions of the program that impinge especially on him. He can, for those particular units, prepare himself in considerable depth and bring to his students that extra sharp edge of scholarship which the public feels they deserve. This is a possibility that merits more thoughtful consideration before the nation stampedes in the general direction of team-teaching. The idea can receive assistance from teacher training

institutions by building the second and third layers of subject matter training into their professional requirements for elementary
majors. Under such a program, the elementary major instead of
having a subject major or minor might have a triple sequence of
courses in some of the fundamental areas that he would be expected to teach, such as language, mathematics, social studies, and
science. The teacher emerging from such a program would still be
broadly prepared as elementary teachers need to be, but he would
have, in addition, an increased level of competence in several basic
areas. It would be a worthy challenge to the colleges of liberal arts
to revise their offerings in such a way that they could provide elementary majors with exciting sequences of this kind. Skillfully
packaged and presented, they might be a major contribution to
teacher education in these troubled times.

The Balanced Program

The range and versatility of the social studies provide an em-
barrassment of riches. Perhaps no one is in a position to describe
what actually amounts to a balanced program, but judging from
mistakes that seem to be perpetuated in the classrooms it may be in
order to suggest five significant aspects of balance which merit consideration. These are as follows:

1. A balance between geography and history. In the schools that
have merged geography and history into a unified program there
may be a tendency for geography to be lost in the shuffle. The
merger is a desirable one for it tends to maximize the natural relationships which exist. Thus, the merger should be maintained, but
geography should continue to be a prominent aspect of the program.

2. A balance between learning from texts and learning from life.
There seems to be no question of the fact that the typical program
is too heavily weighted in the direction of the printed word. Life is
the master text and books, valuable though they may be, are vastly
inferior to their master. A teacher need not attempt to achieve equal
balance in this sense, but he should filter through his program
whatever elements of real life and experience are appropriate and

possible in a given community. Use of the classroom as a laboratory for social living helps to achieve this aspect of balance, and the selective use of resource persons and field study provides an equally valuable assist.

3. *A balance between the present and the past.* History provides the perspective for which there is no substitute; today may be a great deal more meaningful to a child if he understands the yesterdays as well. The relationship is a reciprocal one for the study of yesterday is vitalized when it is mirrored in the context of today. It is a wise teacher who weaves these threads together, skillfully relating the present to the past. A strong current events program beginning in the first year of school and continuing right on through the curriculum is necessary to achieve this type of balance.

4. *A balance between content and process or between the planned experience and the experience of planning.* In the discussion of the selective core of information there was provision for building up and maintaining a more valuable body of content. This is an important qualitative factor, but the learning process itself in which children can be active participants in planning, carrying out, and evaluating some of their own experiences is probably more valuable. If this be true, here again is an instance of imbalance in most programs. This is the motivation for selecting qualitative factors of a definite process-nature such as critical thinking and the development of self-direction.

5. *A balance between intellectual and behavioral goals.* Perhaps the ultimate test of education lies in behavior rather than in mere knowing. A child might verbalize the concept of equality of man and yet in his actions demonstrate a racial arrogance. One must remember that the essence of social studies is human relationships and that the program is not a success unless the quality of living is demonstrably improved. So few programs genuinely nourish attitudes and enlightened human behavior *as an intrinsic part of the program.* Until this is done, social studies remains in the book and never becomes imbedded in the behavior which is its goal.

Balance implies more than the five aspects which have been described. Balance is in a very real sense an attitude itself, and if a school desires to have a balanced program it is armed with the chief instrument for achieving it. Any school, however, that can provide for suitable and adequate expression of these five aspects of balance has done very well and merits a special qualitative praise.

Quality Control

The term quality control is familiar in industry and refers to the means of controlling the quality of the product. It is a term which is descriptive of the idea to be considered here; for the nature of the evaluation may often dictate the nature of the program. If, for instance, a child's grade in social studies is to be determined by a simple test of information, the effect is to ascribe to information an exaggerated importance, so that information for its own sake becomes the key point of the program. The qualitative factors that have been developed in this interpretation, however, indicate that information is only one of the results desired. Over and above facts and skills, one is concerned with a cluster of factors having to do with attitudes and total performance as a thinking and socialized human being. Each of these must receive attention in the evaluation.

With respect to the method of evaluating information or facts, it is probably best for a school to develop its own test. The content of the program varies sufficiently from school to school that the norms from standardized tests are meaningless. As a school works to refine what it regards as a selective core of more essential information, it can also develop items which will evaluate the outcome in this specific aspect of the program. It is perfectly desirable that this be done, but equally desirable to recognize it *as a segment of the evaluation and thus to hold it in perspective.*

The evaluation of social studies skills is more appropriately appraised by using professionally prepared instruments. A test like Test B of the *Iowa Every-Pupil Tests of Basic Skills*[3] evaluates skill in map reading much better than the instruments most teachers could produce on their own. The work-study skills sections of this device evaluate the kinds of social studies skills that all children should develop regardless of the variation of social studies content. The evaluation of such social studies skills constitutes another val-

[3] *Iowa Every-Pupil Tests of Basic Skills,* Boston, Houghton Mifflin, 1955.

uable segment of the total appraisal of the quality product that is sought.

Another constellation of ingredients that should be a significant part of the evaluation has to do with children's attitudes and behavior. This is probably the most important segment of the evaluation, as well as the most neglected. It is best done by on the spot observation by the teacher and is admittedly difficult. It involves recognition of less tangible factors, such as tolerance, fair play, cooperation, careful judgment, and critical thinking.

In instances where this segment is left out of the evaluation it tends also to filter out of the program. A teacher can make the task more manageable for himself and also sharpen his skill in discernment by limiting the factors to be appraised and working at them initially one at a time. Thus, he might for a given period of time concentrate on the observation of demonstrated instances of cooperation, making mental note of those instances and developing a keener awareness of their occurrence. After a satisfactory period of time he might then shift to another of the desirable performance qualities that he seeks to promote and give his special attention to it. By the end of the year he could have quite easily pointed up some very significant instances of desirable behavior in several categories. Thus, he would have given impetus to this desirable segment of the program and would have sharpened his own sensitivity and skill in recognizing and promoting it.

The qualitative program may wish to include in the evaluation more segments than facts, skills, and performance factors, but it cannot afford to include less.

Summary

The discussion has attempted to describe the spirit as well as the substance of an excellent program of social studies and has interpreted eight factors that are believed to be of considerable consequence. The factors are summarized as follows. A qualitative social studies program:

1. Uses the classroom and environs as a laboratory for social living.
2. Stresses its unique opportunities for developing ideals.
3. Highlights a selective core of information.

4. Cultivates critical thinking.
5. Provides gradative experiences in self-direction.
6. Strives for additional depth in its program.
7. Consciously balances its content and methods.
8. Applies the concept of quality control.

Chapter 3

Science in the Elementary School

Science has emerged today as a respected and powerful aspect of the school program. For many years elementary science was regarded as a sort of leaf-pressing, rock-collecting, insect-gathering adjunct to the school day. During this arrested state of development it was interpreted as nature study and was tolerated and even regarded as a nicety; but few people other than nature lovers thought it was of any fundamental importance. Blough and Blackwood were probably trying to break through this attitude when they spoke as follows:

It's not a series of object lessons about a piece of granite, an old wasp's nest, an acorn or tulip. . . . It's not learning the names of the parts of a grasshopper or of a trillium. It's not learning to identify 20 trees, 20 insects, 20 flowers, or 20 anything else.[1]

Attitudes toward science in the curriculum have undergone a drastic change, and today in most informed schools it is likely to enjoy the same attention and esteem that has traditionally been reserved for the three R's. There need be no regret attached to this transition, for science is deserving of a more favored role than it has enjoyed in the past. It has served its time on the bench and belongs now on the varsity. Anyone who has seen the excitement on children's faces in the excellent science class knows how they reach out hungrily for understanding and truth about their world, and what an impetus this can give to the entire tone of the program.

[1] Glenn O. Blough and Paul E. Blackwood, *Teaching Elementary Science*, Bulletin no. 4, Federal Security Agency, U.S. Government Printing Office, Washington, D.C., 1948, p. 2.

Perhaps much of the science program for elementary grades will continue to be based on the immediate environment: trees, insects, stars, clouds, rain, flowers, rocks, and machines are part of the lives of children. They are sources of wonder and beauty and satisfaction. They can contribute richly to a glorious childhood— and they should do so, for there is a time when such important matters need to take place as one grows up. Science, however, is not just stars and clouds and rocks and flowers. It is not even jets and rockets and fuel cells. Science is a way of thinking.

The relationship between elementary science and social studies is an overlapping one. One such overlap is the core function which has traditionally been assigned to the social studies. Science has an equally pervasive quality, and a similar inherent capacity to provide content and inspiration to other areas of the program. In some schools this overlap is recognized by allowing double time for the science unit, and following it with double time for the social studies unit. Thus, the units are taught alternately rather than concurrently, with additional benefit to the core factor.

There is a great deal of folklore surrounding the science area of the curriculum. The chief bit of nonsense which has wide currency among elementary teachers is that science is terribly complicated and difficult. There is no foundation for this belief. In fact, elementary science can be less complicated and difficult than the teaching of either reading or language. Certainly it functions in terms of more orderly and logical principles. Anyone who can master the disorderly array of contradictions that comprise an understanding of the language should find the mastery of basic scientific principles comparatively easy. It is the lack of adequate preparation in science, rather than its inherent difficulty, which seems to create the problem. Most of the following factors should be manageable within the context of the present resources of the school.

Focus on Scientific Thinking

The chief element of quality in science lies in its capacity to develop scientific thinking in children. This forms part of the intent of the science program in most schools, but lacks the degree of emphasis which it requires in order to be effective. It tends to become interwoven with other purposes, and loses some of its strength in the process. The stating of multiple purposes for elementary science, however, tends to obscure the unique and central role to be played by this aspect of the curriculum, thereby weakening its contribution. Its central purpose needs to be clarified, and the position taken here is that the focus is properly and logically placed on scientific thinking itself.

Some professional people believe that this is too restricted a role for science to play. Actually, it would seem to be both a pervading and vital function. To contribute substantially to a child's ability to think scientifically is an accomplishment of the greatest consequence, and can exert a beneficial influence on his personal life as well as being beneficial to the national destiny. The objective can even embrace morality: for truth is one of the respected approaches to morality. Socrates, one of the greatest philosophers produced by western civilization, believed that if one knew (had knowledge) he could not do wrong. Scientific thinking has weakened prejudice and intolerance, and may be one of the chief hopes for a higher level of world morality.

A goal of scientific thinking has reference to mental processes such as observing, comparing, analyzing, generalizing, and problem-solving—all within the reach of children. Such processes have a common denominator. They are all ways of getting at truth, appropriate to different situations and with different degrees of reliability. Scientific thinking is thus regarded as the kind of thinking that may be utilized in the search for truth. Children are keen observers and are quite capable of detecting likenesses and differences. They are able to perform rudimentary analysis, and to generalize after a number of experiences with the same kind of a problem. Their first efforts at problem-solving are scattered and ineffectual but show remarkable improvement by the end of the sixth grade. An excellent groundwork in scientific inquiry can be made in the elementary school if the goal is directed to that end.

This focus is one of the most significant aspects of the modern school, and permeates the program in an unmistakable manner. The teacher who is guided by it works with children in such a way as to awaken and sustain their curiosity. He will listen more than he talks and stimulate more than he answers. He will build into his program those things that are interesting, and will sharpen powers of observation and analysis. He will provide time and resources for pursuing answers to questions asked by the children. He will show respect for truth as well as truth seeking, and will help each child to mature in his ability to approach problems as the true scientist approaches them.

Process Over Content

Investigators have indicated that there is very little agreement on the subject matter of science in the program. Agreement is relatively unnecessary, however, in view of the basic goal of developing scientific thinking. The basic goal is best advanced by processes that strengthen and refine thinking itself, and to some extent any particular content is relatively expendable. There is no reason to believe, for instance, that leaving out any given segment of content such as magnetism and electricity would seriously impair the development of scientific thinking itself. Neither is there any substantial basis for believing that any given segment of the program must be taught at a specific grade or age level. In other words, science as an area of the curriculum is such that content is subordinate to process.

This is a tremendous opportunity which is not enjoyed by most of the other aspects of the program. Teachers in most schools must observe grade level boundaries and sequences in the teaching of reading, mathematics, and even social studies. In science, however, there is still an opportunity to try out and explore different types of content with considerable freedom. Thus, creative teachers may enjoy the special luxury of pursuing with children the real interests they have about their amazing world, with attention devoted only to improving the processes of their thought.

It seems reasonable to point out that schools have not taken advantage of this freedom and that they have not adequately attempted to develop scientific processes as such. Very few schools seem to have stated boldly and unequivocally to their teachers that this process of freedom and emphasis exists in elementary science. This must be so stated, because teachers by and large are so preoccupied with content that they seem to have a giant fixation on it. Thus, to shake content loose from its traditional moorings, active administrative encouragement is required.

The subordination of content must be accompanied by a corresponding emphasis of the kinds of instructional activities that are rich in promoting the desired goals. This should be the focus of curriculum development in science instead of the present exaggerated concern over what should be taught at which grade level. The school should build into its program those activities which afford more of a maximum opportunity for observing, comparing, analyzing, generalizing, and problem-solving. Environmental study seems rich in possibilities, and so also is experimentation, or what some prefer to call "experiences with phenomena." More experiences of this nature should be carefully fused through the teaching of science, for there is ample evidence of the fact that the incidence of this kind of activity is not commensurate with the need. Strangely enough, the schools that have built such activities into their program have been punished for doing so. They have frequently been forced into a psychological mood to retrench as a result of carping criticisms and demands that they return to the three R's. There is no reason to believe that the activity in question is detrimental to the three R's. There is considerable reason to believe the contrary; that the relationship is symbiotic and that a judicious emphasis of process in science would actually stimulate them.

The factor under discussion at this point, however, has to do with freeing the teacher from the pressure of any particular content burden in science so that scientific thinking may enjoy the priority which it deserves. The recognition and emphasis of this concept is a necessary condition of the qualitative approach.

Functional Extension of Learnings

The fact that an area of the curriculum accepts the major responsibility for developing scientific thinking gives it an additional function. The process is nurtured and receives special direction in a basic core of experiences provided within the program; but it must be extended and applied additionally throughout the curriculum if it is to be effective. In other words, if scientific thinking were to receive emphasis in the science class and then remain suspended until the next science period, the goal would be seriously compromised and the program crippled. Growth in the kind of thinking sought in science is a part of one's mental processes. It cannot be turned on and off like an electric current for it becomes imbedded in the personality of the individual. Thus, the habits of curiosity and truth seeking require a freer and more meaningful expression, and must be able to function throughout the school day.

There are some interesting and challenging ramifications to this extension. The same truth seeking process that probes into rainbows, humming birds, and chlorophyl will probe into other aspects of the curriculum as well. School personnel must be oriented to live with this curiosity, to direct it as best they can, and to search with children for the most reliable sources of information that can be found.

Sometimes the questions will move into an area that is believed to be the exclusive domain of adults. "Why do we do our arithmetic with laborious hand and mental methods when the real world of business and industry uses machines? Why do we claim that seven types of food are necessary for a balanced diet and health when some of the healthiest specimens on the globe simply do not eat them? Why do we write spelling words in lists when the real use of spelling is in the expression of thoughts?" Such questions should be answered, and if there are no good answers the practices should be revised. This is tremendously important—for anything less does not show a respect for truth.

Some of the questions children ask are humorous as well as provocative. One fifth grade boy asked why people spoke of dressing a chicken when they were in fact undressing it. The same boy called attention to the unusual logic displayed by women in wearing their fur coats with the fur "outside." Bright elementary school children have been known to ask why war must continue to threaten the world when people themselves do not seem to want war, and why there is so much hunger in a world with so much surplus food.

Asking their questions and searching together for the best possible answers stimulate and realistically extend the kind of thinking which is the primary goal of the science program. So long as science is regarded as a way of thinking, it must also be regarded as a way of life. It cannot be achieved within the science period alone. The excellent teacher develops a special sensitivity or awareness of opportunities to extend the science learnings within the classroom. This functional extension is an essential one and is one of the important marks of quality of the excellent elementary school.

Science Oriented Teachers

At this point it might be well to bring to the surface a rather candid question. Can a nonscience oriented teacher produce science oriented children? Perhaps he can, but it does not seem to be a very realistic assumption.

Suppose that a teacher is somewhat slovenly in his thought patterns, that he uses language loosely rather than precisely, that he depends too much on his textbooks, that he is complacent about what he knows and has no real desire to extend his present horizons. Suppose that he reasons in stereotypes, clichés, and prejudices which he is unwilling to examine; that he is intolerant of questions which contain a hint of challenge or disbelief, and feels the thinking has already been done and it is the job of children only to memorize. Can such a man teach science as a way of thinking? Can he by any stretch of the imagination demonstrate through his own behavior the extension of scientific thinking throughout other portions of the school day?

The question may involve the kind of academic background possessed by the teacher, but goes beyond it to the kind of person he happens to be. It is perhaps primarily a personality factor, for there are many rigid, inflexible, nonscientific "scientists" as well as many open-minded, flexible, scientifically oriented laymen. The matter seems to be of considerable importance, for this is obviously an age in which science learnings must be refined and intensified; and the entire process could be defeated by failing to provide the right kind of classroom leadership. The point is equally valid and critical in the social studies, but was not discussed in order to avoid repetition. Obviously, the characteristics of excellence sought in the social studies could not find expression under the custody of an intolerant and narrow-minded teacher. Not a single one of the selective factors could flourish in such a setting.

The problem is compounded by the fact that money will not solve it. Higher salaries are just as attractive to the dull as to the thinkers. For the individual school the problem is at least partially subject to control. The values of the culture are such that good classroom teachers are much less in demand than a successful coach; and so the school that knows what it wants can generally go out and find it. The writer is acquainted with schools that consistently reach out and attract the best teachers, even though they may not pay the highest salaries. They wisely devote extra effort to this, for the school that wishes to provide the best possible environment for its children will make a major effort to get the very finest teachers.

Science and Personality

Science has an important relationship and contribution to make to the developing personality of children. Haan has called attention to the manner in which the teaching of science could diminish a child's sense of trust:

We can teach day and night in a way to show precision and certainty of the earth's turning in space; we can also teach that we are hurtling through space in a nameless void at incredible speeds with unknown dangers at every turn.[2]

It is doubtful that many of us are sufficiently imaginative and articulate enough to produce the sophisticated interpretation above, but the point that many aspects of science can be taught in such a way as to arouse either fear or trust is well made.

A second aspect of science and personality has to do with a child's drive toward it. Most adults can recognize a teacher whose relationship to children is too sticky. Sometimes such a teacher is unconsciously exploiting children as a result of her own unfulfilled emotional needs. A somewhat similar condition may also prevail between science and an individual child. Kubie has called attention to this in outlining the process through which a young scientist may have selected his vocation.[3] A gifted child develops some neurotic tendencies which inhibit his normal psychosexual development. He is intellectually stimulated by some esteemed adult and turns to books. Finding that success follows these efforts he

[2] Aubrey Haan, *Elementary Curriculum: Theory and Research,* Boston, Allyn and Bacon, 1961, p. 215.
[3] Lawrence S. Kubie, "Some Unsolved Problems of the Scientific Career, Part I," American Scientist, XLI (1953), no. 4.

may restrict himself to intellectual activity during adolescence. The physical and emotional drain of laboratory time can also result in one's putting all his emotional eggs in the intellectual basket. His sense of security and self-esteem come to stand on one leg. When original research finally begins, it is supercharged with many irrelevant and unfulfilled emotional needs.

It would seem that the school has a guidance function to exercise in cases of this kind, even if in the process the world stands to lose a scientist. Sometimes science seems to overobjectify a person and to factor out basic qualities of human warmth. This is more than a personal tragedy for today the world needs compassion and maturity from its scientists even more than it needs their remarkable achievements.

In a more general personality sense an excellent science program can help children to become more resourceful and less naïve, more confident and less cocky, more deliberate and less hurried, and more capable of surmounting an unpredictable tomorrow. This potential seems inadequately explored. If a given experience in science can contribute to the major goal and also be presented in such a way as to exert a constructive and wholesome influence on children's lives, it is desirable that it be done. A personality emphasis is implied in the acceptance of scientific thinking as the focus of the program. This additional factor is derived from the central purpose and simply gives an additional dimension to the concept.

The Science of Health

Health is a part of the curriculum in most elementary schools today. Sometimes it is combined with safety as one of the six major segments of the program, and sometimes it is merged with science. The inclusion of health and safety here as a part of the excellent science program is in no sense an attempt to minimize their importance, for each is a vital part of the curriculum and must certainly be maintained. This interpretation of health as one of the proper concerns of science is suggested because it seems logical and natural. Health is dependent upon science and in many respects is a product of science. Science has eradicated many of the major diseases that have plagued mankind, and is the chief beacon of hope for eradicating those that remain. From science has come, also, the most reliable principles that man has for building and maintaining his health.

It is widely reported and believed that the nation's youth are less fit than one could expect them to be, and the rate of rejection by the military services is cited as evidence of this condition. Could it be that one of the factors responsible for this condition is the rather infantile approach to health in many schools? Health education in many ways seems to be persuasive rather than insightful, its influence transitory rather than constant, and verbalisms about health somehow fail to take root in one's pattern of living.

As one develops science in the elementary school as a way of thinking, this thoughtful process of inquiry should embrace healthful living as one of its legitimate and major targets. There are at least three ways to move in this direction. One is to include in the science units for the year at least one which is health focused. A second way is to scan each science unit that is developed for whatever ramifications and generalizations it holds for healthful living and to point them up in process. A third, and perhaps most powerful approach, is to utilize scientific thinking on incidental problems of healthful living whenever they occur in the classroom. This approach seems most potentially rewarding because it is closer to the goal of making health a matter of behavior rather than a subject to be studied.

Too many young people today casually take up smoking and drinking and even drug addiction. This social cancer has now moved down into the elementary grades. No single factor can be expected to remove a social tragedy of this dimension, but health as a strong and vital adjunct to the science program has a contributing role to play. The qualitative science curriculum will, therefore, include the science of health as one of the primary aspects of its program.

The Science of Safety

What has been said about the science of health applies equally well to the science of safety, and the rationale for its inclusion need not be repeated.

One classroom approaches this problem in the following way. The teacher and the class study their school environment for accident-laden situations. They carefully observe these situations, thoughtfully discuss and analyze them, and then propose what seem to be the most promising means of eliminating or guarding against them. Notice how closely the procedure parallels the approach of the scientist, and how such thinking has been directed at a realistic and vital problem that is of genuine concern to the participants.

Each time a major accident occurs, the routine machinery of the classroom comes to a halt and the accident comes to the top of the agenda. The class may go out to the scene of the accident for first-hand investigation, and then come back to their room where the sequence and conditions are reenacted. The children attempt to analyze the cause and to make suitable recommendations. The process is calm, objective, and analytical. It is scientific thinking in action directed at a highly meaningful situation in the children's own lives.

The same class engages in a somewhat comparable approach that has strong appeal to the children. An identification is made of the chief causes of death and accidents to children generally and in the local community. Suppose, for example, that one such cause is a situation where a child is running from a playground, behind a parked car, and then suddenly in front of an oncoming automobile. This situation is portrayed in the classroom with actual materials which show the playground, the parked car, the children playing, and the approaching automobile. A child sets up the arrangement, which contains a potentially dangerous situation, and the children think through it and discuss it. Later, they may invite in a class of younger children and portray it for them. The careful identification of the kinds of accidents which are real hazards to children is an important part of the approach, and introduces a vital type of content in the program.

As in the case of health, the science of safety as a concern of the program provides impetus and functional use of scientific thinking directed at one of the paramount problems of children's existence. It is thus appropriately included in the context of the qualitative school.

Evaluation

In keeping with the primary focus of science the evaluation is directed at the children themselves and how they think. Observation is probably the most valuable guide to this process. As the authors of one major text put it: "There is scarcely any legitimate reason for using standardized tests in elementary science." [4]

One evaluates what he has been trying to achieve, and in the case of any given child the evaluation might reasonably be concerned with matters such as the following:

1. Is he more interested and curious?
2. Is he more open-minded?
3. Is he more observing and analytical?
4. Is he more able to generalize?
5. Is he more sensitive to causality?
6. Is he more resourceful in his attack of problems?
7. Is he more careful about the sources of his information and more tentative in his conclusions?
8. Is he more scientific in his pursuit of learning beyond the science class itself?

An especially rich evaluative practice is that of having children evaluate themselves on questions such as those above. It is particularly effective when the class has cooperatively determined what they are striving for, and have pinned it down in terms that are meaningful to them. A group form of this type of evaluation is also possible. It takes place when the teacher has set up a problem which is carefully interpreted. The teacher then steps aside while the children, entirely on their own, advance, discuss, and interpret their hypotheses. The teacher then returns to more active participation and all of them thoughtfully evaluate what they have done.

Another rich possibility for special observation occurs when a class puts on a demonstration or experiment for another group. Following such an activity they will then evaluate the strengths and

[4] Glenn Blough, *et al.*, *Elementary School Science and How to Teach It*, rev. ed., New York, The Dryden Press, 1951, p. 84.

weaknesses of their presentation. The teacher's function here is best carried out when he carefully hears out the children themselves before advancing any of his own evaluative remarks.

Such activities have a special inherent strength. Critical thinking is present in each, and thus the evaluative process itself exemplifies the spirit and intent of the program.

Summary

Elementary science can contribute one of the most valued aspects of a child's development if it successfully identifies and maintains its central focus. No other aspect of the curriculum has a more vital role to play in equipping the child to live in a world that is bound to become increasingly complex and technical. The central focus of science is best nourished in a series of planned experiences that emphasize process over content and give children real experiences in guided forms of scientific inquiry. These forms of scientific thinking are then additionally strengthened by extended applications throughout the rest of the school program. Regardless of the degree and kind of content which he may master, the child who has learned science as a way of thinking has a start in life which should serve him well. Eight factors of excellence were interpreted. The qualitative program will be one which:

1. Accepts scientific thinking as its major goal.
2. Emphasizes process over content.
3. Provides for functional extension of learnings.
4. Attempts to select science oriented teachers.
5. Contributes positively to personality development.
6. Teaches the science of health.
7. Teaches the science of safety.
8. Keeps its evaluation directed at the major goal.

Chapter 4

Language Usage

Across the length and breadth of the land an articulate chorus of voices complains that today's youth are grossly deficient in their ability to use language effectively. Even if one assumed that much of the current criticism is exaggerated and misinformed it is still apparent that schools have not yet turned in their best effort to develop good usage. Most people learn only one language in a lifetime. It seems reasonable to expect that they should learn it well.

Some of the complications associated with an attempt to improve usage are pointed up by Dawson in a review of 45 years of research on the teaching of language usage.[1] She draws from an interesting background of evidence to indicate that many of the cherished beliefs about how to get the job done are not at all promising.

For instance, most people regard the teaching of grammar to be a solid and respectable approach to improved usage, yet the Hoyt study found the correlation to be as low as 0.12 to 0.23 which is no correlation at all.[2] This lack of relationship is further indicated in a study by Boraas who found additionally that knowledge of grammar correlated better with knowledge of history and arithmetic than with the ability to speak and write effectively.[3]

[1] Mildred A. Dawson, "Summary of Research Concerning English Usage," *Elementary English,* XXVIII (March, 1951), 141–147.
[2] F. S. Hoyt, "The Place of Grammar in the Elementary Curriculum," *Teachers College Record,* VII (November, 1906), 467–500.
[3] Julius Boraas, *Formal English Grammar and the Practical Mastery of English,* Ph.D. Thesis, University of Minnesota, 1917.

Ortmeyer studied the teaching of rules to eighth graders and discovered that a pupil could know the rule and yet use the incorrect form, or conversely, that he could use the correct form and not know the rule.[4] There was a correlation of only 0.51 between grammatical knowledge and the ability to write without serious error.

As the pendulum swings back today to what is fondly believed by so many adults to be the tried and true there is a renewed interest in diagramming. The same lack of correlation exists here, however, and diagramming seems merely to improve the ability to diagram.[5] It does not improve one's ability to write or speak more effectively.

The basic meaning of the Dawson summary is simply that the teaching of formal grammar is not an effective approach to the problem. This shocks many parents, angers many grammerians, and confuses many teachers for their reliance on the grammar approach has been out of all proportion to the evidence as to what it can achieve. Pooley speaks to the unwarranted reliance on grammar as follows:

This fallacy arises from the assumption that an error in a verb form (he done it) is corrected by teaching the pupil the principal parts of the verb to do; or that a pronoun error (him and me went home) is corrected by teaching the declension of the pronoun. The approach to correctness through grammar may have some validity for the adult who has developed the power to reason and arrive at conclusions from particular instances. For the young child, however, the evidence is definitely negative. . . . The teaching of grammatical forms will contribute essentially nothing to the improvement of children's speech habits.[6]

One must always be cautious of the conclusions formed from research, even as he must be careful of opinions that are formed without the benefit of research. New approaches to grammar may be devised and may prove to be more rewarding. At the present time, however, there seems to be no substantial basis for a heavy emphasis of grammar in *the elementary school*. Like an investor

[4] W. A. Ortmeyer, *The Relation of Mastery of Certain Punctuation Rules to Pupil Usage*, M.A. Thesis, University of Iowa, 1932.

[5] James R. Stewart, *The Effect of Diagramming on Certain Skills in English Composition*, Ph.D. Thesis, University of Iowa, 1941.

[6] Robert C. Pooley, *Teaching English Usage*, New York, Appleton–Century–Crofts, 1946, pp. 181–182.

who seeks to avoid committing too much of his capital to a stock yielding a poor return, the school must develop a more diversified portfolio. Six factors bearing on a better balanced and more qualitative approach are suggested in the following remarks about this vital aspect of the program.

The Enlightened Setting

Perhaps everyone at some time in his life has been in a classroom where he didn't dare to express an idea for if he did it would be chopped off. It doesn't take much chopping off to create a psychological wasteland with a conspicuous absence of ideas.

Perhaps everyone at some time in his life has been in a group where one of the members in a moment of spontaneity beautifully captured the spirit of an idea, and someone took the life out of it by correcting his English.

Perhaps everyone has at some time or another been in a class when the entire group seemed to come alive on an idea and wished to discuss it, but the teacher hurried on to the next point.

Perhaps everyone in his lifetime has seen a child groping for just the right way to express something when a precipitate adult supplied it for him, effectively shutting off any further thought.

Perhaps everyone has read or written a theme full of feeling, imagination, and color that was red-penciled all over by someone who long ago had lost his capacity for feeling, imagination, and color.

And then perhaps everyone has wondered why at age six the child is so full of ideas and the desire to express them and at sixteen he is so dehydrated.

An enlightened setting is simple and unpretentious. It is a place where interesting things happen that are worth writing and talking about. It is a place where one is encouraged to express his ideas, and then is made to feel that what one has to say is worth listening to. It is a place where the tables are turned and the children talk a little more and the teacher talks a little less. It is a place where a good dose of freedom is the sunshine, thoughtfulness is the rich, black earth, and incentive is the rain.

There is a comfortable feeling in such a classroom. One doesn't have to convey all of his thoughts as though he were addressing a joint session of Congress. One doesn't have to speak like a stuffed shirt in a manner which is unnatural to his way of life and alien to his peer group. This is one of the refreshing differences of the modern school. In the old days there was a stilted twist to correct usage that restricted the quality of its development. The modern linguist recognizes the psychology of a situation and its relationship to correctness of speech. Thus, the circumstances determine whether it is more appropriate to say "Beat it!" or "Please go." Obviously, it is improper to wear one's fatigues to a ball; but it is equally improper to wear a tuxedo to a track meet. It is the latter concept which the old style grammarian has been so reluctant to concede. Some have been so pristine and sterile in their approach that they have almost destroyed the demand for their product. It is no wonder that many young people rejected a concept of language which was so separated from life. The adaptation of language to the circumstances in which it is used adds to the sensitivity and richness of expression, and gives it a greater range. It is somewhat like the adjustment of music to mood. A significant segment of realism has been added and the language is improved. It is more virile and attractive to young learners and more worthy of their efforts to achieve. No one but a fool would announce that he was going to bed by saying, "I shall withdraw to seek repose."

Such elements of comfort and realism, however, are not to be construed as a license to leave things as they are. It is more of a license to be enlightened about what is appropriate, and the kinds of improvements that should be sought. Tension and anxiety are reduced but thinking is increased, and thinking is directed at improvements in the language used. The enlightened setting then is a comfortable one, a realistic one, and an interesting one—but one with a growing edge.

Realistic Goals

Stuart Little is the title of a delightful book which should probably be read by all children as well as by most adults. Stuart is a tiny boy, born in the shape of a mouse, to two otherwise perfectly normal parents. In one passage Stuart has asked a bird, appropriately named Margalo, where she is from. Then comes this splendid line:

I come from fields once tall with wheat, from pastures deep in fern and thistle. I come from vales of meadowsweet, and I love to whistle.[7]

Margalo, a mere bird, has spoken at a very high level of literary expression. Her words are simple and expressive, and they fall together in such a way as to create beauty and imagery. Few adults ever achieve this level of expression. What are the goals which one might realistically expect of children?

Grammarians usually recognize five levels of usage which merge together in such a way that they cannot be clearly separated. One is known as the illiterate level and is completely outside the boundaries of acceptability. This level is reflected by expressions such as, *you is, I seed, he knowed,* etc. The language program of a cultivated society will strive to eliminate this level entirely.

A notch or so above the illiterate level is one which is very touchy and is called the homely level. It may be characterized by such expressions as *whip cream, light-complected girl, I reckon,* and *Mary, she.* This one is touchy because some element of it is a part of the speech patterns of many worthy men and women, and most children are likely to hear such usages in their own homes. The language program of the elementary school must try to eliminate this level also, but must do so with great kindness and tact.

The third and fourth levels constitute that broad range of acceptable usage known as standard English. Its lower extremity, called informal standard, should be the normal usage of the elementary classroom and the goal set for most pupils to attain. It is a comfortable type of usage of the kind that might characterize the relaxed and informal conversation of cultured persons. It is not satisfactory, however, for more formal talks and written work. The upper level of this range, known as formal standard, is the goal for carefully prepared written work, prepared talks, and formal correspondence. A formal standard level is more selective in choice of words, more attentive to word order, and more careful about such matters as case and number agreement.

At the top of the mountain is the highest level of all. It is called the literary level, and it beckons many but is attained by only a few. It is a form of writing or speaking which goes beyond mere communication to achieve beauty. Lincoln's Gettysburg Address is

[7] E. B. White, *Stuart Little,* New York, Harper & Brothers, 1945, p. 51.

a classic example of this level of language. Those who achieve it are exceptionally gifted in their vocabulary, are likely to have an unusual sensitivity to how words fit together to create a desired effect, and are able to transcend utility to achieve beauty, as did Margalo in her reply to Stuart. Children cannot be expected to achieve the literary level of language, nor, indeed, can most of their teachers.

No aspect of the curriculum is more in need of realistic goals than language usage. The child who comes to the doors of the school with six years of illiterate or homely usage ringing in his ears has a great struggle ahead of him to achieve even the lower rungs of acceptance and respectability. He needs massive doses of patience, incentive, and encouragement. His goal must be set where he can reach it. It is all right to make him stretch a bit, but having stretched and having tried, the goal must be within his reach. He must never be made to feel awkward and unworthy because of his language, and when he has tried his very best, his best must always be regarded as good enough. Any other approach to such a child is morally and professionally wrong.

At the other end of the continuum is the child who is twice blessed. He comes to school with six years of good usage patterns woven through his language. His parents have listened to him attentively and given him all possible encouragement. He is confident and poised. In the first two years of elementary school he moves perceptibly into the informal standard level at the early age of eight. The goal must be different for him; there is no other sensible way.

For the child at either end and for all those in between, the goal must fit like an expertly tailored suit. Choose the size and the color and the fabric with care. Don't hang a thirty-eight jacket on a skinny little guy. Don't put a bulky tweed on a child who is already too fat. Don't put a faded color on a hollow-cheeked little girl. Make it fit every child in the room. That's the realistic note in goals.

Priority Content

Some aspects of the curriculum lend themselves more readily to the determination of a small body of information which is very desirable and even vital to learn. This is true for instance of spelling, where research has identified a relatively small number of words that account for a relatively high proportion of the total words used. It is also true of English usage, where the constant repetition of a small number of errors may account for 90 percent of the usage problem in the elementary grades.

The basic idea of priority content is of course to focus effort where it will do the most good. In the total picture, major responsibility for certain types of errors would be assigned to the elementary school, others to the Jr. high school, and the more complex and advanced considerations would be reserved for the high schools and universities.

Pooley has prepared such a list or inventory of items for the elementary grades, and has even prepared additionally a list of items which he does not believe to be appropriate for emphasis at the elementary level. Those which he would recommend for special attention in grades one through six are as follows:

Errors to Be Eliminated in the Elementary School[8]

ain't, or hain't	he give	he run
hair are	I got for I've got	have saw
a orange	my brother, he (and	I says
have ate	other double sub-	he seen
he begun	jects)	them books
was broke	her, him and me	theirselves
he brung	went	this here
climb (short i)	hisself	that there
clumb	there is, was four	us boys went
he come	knowed; growed, etc.	we, you, they was
have did	learn me a song	with we girls
he, she, it don't	leave me go	have went
I drunk	me and Mary went	have wrote
didn't hadn't	haven't no, haven't	it is yourn, hern, ourn,
ought	nothing	theirn
was froze		

The list of errors to be corrected at this level deliberately omits many of the usage errors that are included in workbooks and texts. This is partially due to the fact that many usages commonly regarded as errors are in the opinion of Pooley not errors at all, but are instead forms of expression which are appropriate to the speech

[8] Robert C. Pooley, *Teaching English Usage*, New York, Appleton–Century–Crofts, p. 180. Copyright © 1946, by Appleton–Century–Crofts.

and writing of young children. It is due, also, to the fact that the list is deliberately restricted to those items which are of the greatest importance to emphasize in the elementary grades. It is thus a more narrow band of the spectrum which is regarded as being within the responsibility of the elementary school, and such content is vulnerable to an effective approach.

This qualitative factor seems disarmingly simple and the reader might reasonably assume that it is a matter which would be automatically provided for in the preparation of study materials for elementary children. One study by Pooley, however, indicated that the texts leave a great deal to be desired in this respect.[9] He took 179 important items of usage and studied eight different text series to determine how many of the 179 items were covered in common by each of the eight texts. Incredible as it seems, only two of the 179 items were so covered. Furthermore, even if all necessary items are in the text material that a school happens to use, the priority items may be lost in the maze of total text content so that they are not selectively highlighted as they would seem to deserve. This is a powerful enough factor that a school simply cannot afford to leave to chance. The qualitative program will take special care to identify its priority content.

Cooperative Analysis and Attack

Using the priority content suggested in the preceding discussion, the teacher moves quickly to establish a cooperative approach to the task of pointing up the most common errors made by the class. This follows a sequence of (1) developing an understanding on the part of the class of which items are on the must list, (2) enlisting their active support in determining which of the errors are made in their own work, (3) establishing some mechanical provision for keeping a record of the results, (4) giving this record a prominent physical and psychological place in the room, and (5) organizing the errors into a priority sequence for attack.

Suppose, for instance, that in the first few days of careful observation and analysis the class and teacher working together have

[9] Robert C. Pooley, *The Teaching of English in Wisconsin,* University of Wisconsin Press, Madison, Wisconsin, 1948, p. 48.

pointed up ten flagrant errors that are commonly made by members of the class. The most intolerable of these errors is selected as target number 1. Then the focus of class activity in the language program is directed at this error in a concerted and all out effort to stamp it out of existence. The initial emphasis is upon understanding the correct form, followed by opportunities to select the right over the wrong form in specific paired choices. Then comes the power punch which is a follow-through of thoughtful attention to written and spoken expression throughout the entire day. Wherever the error occurs it is pounced upon. It has no diplomatic immunity if it occurs in science, mathematics, or physical education. The attack is in the nature of hot pursuit and represents a genuine overall effort to achieve the desired result. After error number 1 is in full state of withdrawal or retreat, the focus shifts to error number 2.

There is considerable strength in the approach just described. Dawson has indicated that much of the teaching of language usage is ineffective because of the following mistakes:

1. Attempting to cover too many errors.
2. Attempting to change usages that are actually acceptable forms of expression.
3. Drilling on items that are in the workbook whether or not those particular errors are made by the class.[10]

The approach suggested overcomes each of these common shortcomings. It controls and limits the errors to be attacked, it selects its targets from a category of genuine problem items, and it focuses only upon the errors that are actually made by the children involved. Furthermore, it makes a total effort which is cooperatively derived. Skillfully delivered, it is capable of altering even entrenched forms of objectionable usage.

Developing a Love of Language

Up to this point, the discussion has been concerned primarily with the less important side of the coin. Analysis of errors, selection of targets, and effective methods of attack are essentially negative

[10] Mildred A. Dawson, "A Summary of Research Concerning English Usage," *Elementary English,* 28 (March, 1951), pp. 141–147.

matters directed at the eradication of objectionable types of usage. What is not generally recognized, however, is that one might remove all the errors from language and still not have good language. Freed from all of its undesirable forms it might still be sterile and unimaginative, lacking in color and warmth, and essentially uninviting. To shift into a forward gear and build into usage the positive elements it should possess is discussed by some as the development of language appreciation. The writer does not care for the term appreciation. One may appreciate the garbage collector without feeling any particular warmth for him. The young learner should have more of a "crush" on language, this mysterious lady who serves us all so well. He should reach out to her, embrace her, and make love to her.

The state of loving implies warmth; language needs warmth. It suggests a quality of vibrant living; vibrant living causes language to come alive. It conveys adequacy, sensitivity, inspiration, pouring out, and giving—language needs all these things. Less than that is simply not enough. How does one promote such a relationship?

One thing that a teacher can do is to show his own love for the lady in thought and deed. When something is said by a child in a child's way and it is said just right—he holds it up for all to see and enjoy. When in their reading the children come across a delightful passage that says just what everyone would like to say in just the way they would have liked to say it—they hold it up for all to see and enjoy. The hurry and the bustle and the driving machinery of onwardness is all temporarily suspended for the sake of enjoyment, just as one would stop to marvel at a rainbow or a flash of lightning in the sky. The teacher shows by his actions that he places a premium on these things. He helps children to sense the beauty of language and to be sensitive to it when it appears.

He teaches them to be proud of their thoughts and to want to clothe them adequately and appropriately with words. A fine thought expressed shabbily is like wearing soiled underwear.

He teaches them to bring color into their language and to express their thoughts in such a way that people really want to hear what they have to say. Then, he shows them how to do this by speaking to them in such a way that they want to hear him.

Day by day he reacts sensitively to the bits of color and the kind of weave that create a comfortable and lovely garment one is proud to wear. This is the forward gear, the positive element, the development of a love for language, and it is the most conspicuous and vital element of an excellent program.

Vocabulary Development

Many of the products of learning do not seem to have any direct relationship either to one's success in life or to his personal happiness. It would be difficult for instance to demonstrate that skill in spelling or computation has any marked effect on one's salary or social position. This is not true, however, of vocabulary development. An excellent vocabulary is one of the educated man's most prized possessions. It has a personal value in making and keeping friends, in sucessfully meeting the hurdles of college and university standards of excellence, and in getting a job and winning promotions. There are few important aspects of modern life that are not in some measure affected by this achievement.

The relationship between intelligence and vocabulary is a positive one. Individuals with high intelligence are likely also to have large vocabularies, and in some psychological tests the vocabulary section has the highest correlation with the total score. There is also an interesting relationship between vocabulary and the level of one's position. Some of the highest scores on tests of vocabulary are made by the top level executives of business and industry. Top executives outscore junior executives and even outscore college and university professors. Top executives seem, also, to make the high scores whether or not they have had a college education.

The elementary school has so many responsibilities that it is certainly understandable when some of its larger tasks tend to be put aside for more expedient matters. Thus, vocabulary development in many schools may not be receiving the degree of emphasis which it deserves. Somehow the qualitative school must manage to keep this factor near the top of its agenda, for the stakes are high and nothing influences language usage as much as the right word in the right place at the right time.

In the primary grades the emphasis on vocabulary continues to be through direct experience. A child in first grade probably has a speaking vocabulary of 2500 words when he enters school. He developed this vocabulary through direct experiences of seeing, hearing, feeling, tasting, and smelling. His teachers build upon this and extend it. They provide additional firsthand experiences which are used for further language growth. For instance, in an enlightened primary room the firsthand experience is carefully discussed and then recorded. First graders will dictate to the teacher what they wish to record about the experience and these stories may be used as a basis for some of their reading. The language is at the linguistic level of maturity of the children for it is their language. It is of course much richer and more advanced than the language of their basic reading series which has a very carefully controlled vocabulary. Words from the recorded experiences are studied and the total vocabulary is strengthened more than it could be strengthened by basal readers alone.

With older children the approach can be more structured. Structural analysis teaches children the root words and their derivations. The child begins to develop some independence in increasing his store of words. He may keep a record of new words which he finds attractive, and wishes to add to those which he already knows. Teachers deliberately use colorful and effective new words to add to their store of meanings. The value and function of the dictionary is taught as an additional tool for developing independence.

Language activity in the classroom constantly reflects the importance of words and their essential role in the adequate expression of one's thoughts. When nature or circumstances have created a special mood it is used to add to the richness of language. Thus, a gentle rain or a new fallen snow may precipitate talking or writing about the feelings that it inspires, and there is an effort to describe feelings with sensitivity and beauty. Words that are overused are replaced with others that are better and more meaningful. Words that ascribe meanings too loosely are replaced with others that have a rapier function. The child's language is stretched. He is taught in such a way as to add new meanings to old words as well as to add new words for new meanings.

In vocabulary development there is no substitute for wide reading. Wide reading alone will expand the child's vocabulary, but wide reading plus the kinds of assistance that have been described will add a kind of additional power and strength to the gains that are made. The expansion of vocabulary is accomplished in part by deliberately invoked procedures in the school. If the school can also develop in the child the desire to add to his store of words on his own, then he would seem to be on his way. He will find for the remainder of his life that this achievement can serve him well. His language usage will have more range and depth, it will be more stimulating and colorful, and he will be more capable of doing justice to his thoughts.

Summary

The discussion of language has attempted to create the image of a program that moves out of the workbook and into children's lives. It is an image that prizes warmth, and color, and spontaneity in expression—to both child and teacher. It is an image that would reach as high as children can go in adequately clothing their thoughts, but it would never ask of a child something that his personal endowments make it impossible for him to give. The image is practical yet creative, sensitive and delicate yet poised and powerful, down in the world of reality where one must live yet adequate to reflect whatever he may aspire to become. Six factors are suggested as being significant. Thus the excellent program is one which:

1. Establishes an enlightened setting.
2. Sets realistic goals.
3. Stresses its priority content.
4. Organizes a cooperative analysis and attack.
5. Develops a love of language.
6. Places a special emphasis upon vocabulary development.

Chapter 5

Language Tools

In the "good old days" the spelling bee was a fairly substantial segment of the social life of a community and handwriting was regarded as one of the distinctive characteristics of a cultivated person. Their status is lower today. The best of handwriting appears somewhat crude in comparison with a beautifully typed letter, and the spelling bees which remain are somewhat artificially contrived. They have passed away like the old-fashioned box suppers which offered to the lucky buyer the additional fringe benefits of the companionship of the lady who had prepared it. Another of the simple, wholesome aspects of an earlier day has disappeared and one cannot help feeling a twinge of nostalgia at the loss.

Spelling and handwriting are skills which are brought into play for expressing ideas in written form; they are tools of communication. Although they no longer enjoy the esteem and place in the program that they once held, they are still important even though they are, admittedly, a minor part of the curriculum.

Spelling may possibly function at the same intellectual level as language usage, but handwriting is more of a mechanical skill. One invokes his brain in spelling, but his handwriting is a habituated form of motor activity. Perhaps this is one of the reasons why handwriting seems to deteriorate with advanced levels of education or achievement. An early study indicated that the illegibilities of high school students exceeded the illegibilities of elementary students by 136%. The illegibilities of adults, however, rose additionally to

350%.[1] A recent journal graphically portrayed the point that the higher one rises in status the less legible his signature becomes.[2] As a young naval officer the signature that was reproduced was quite legible. As a United States senator the signature of the same young man was less legible. As President of the United States, however, the signature was almost unrecognizable. The signature was that of John F. Kennedy. The journal noted that a Harvard well-wisher had spent $3 to enroll President Kennedy (without President Kennedy's knowledge) in a handwriting correspondence school.

The current criticism of young people's spelling is probably deserved and the schools can do a better job than has been done. What may be overlooked, however, is that no adequate data is readily available to reveal precisely how the spelling of people today compares with the achievements of years past. Perhaps the spotlight of attention focuses more brightly on the errors made today than on yesterday. Certainly some very distinguished men of the past made overt errors in spelling. The writing of Lincoln revealed common misspellings even though this great man achieved such a remarkable level of literary usage.

The writer must confess a general partiality to spelling because of the higher intellectual level at which it may function. With so many more vital matters at stake it is unrealistic to become preoccupied with handwriting. One should write legibly and there are well established procedures for doing so. It poses no great challenge. The biggest obstacle today to its highest potential achievement is misguided parents, as will be interpreted in later remarks having to do with the qualitative factors.

The Core Vocabulary of Spelling

Spelling is one of the few aspects of the curriculum for which research can provide a reasonably specific picture of what should be taught. The many studies that have been made on word usage indicate that some words appear more frequently in the written

[1] T. Ernest Newland, "An Analytical Study of the Development of Illegibilities in Handwriting from the Lower Grades to Adulthood," *Journal of Educational Research*, 26 (December, 1932), 249–258.
[2] *Reader's Digest*, Pleasantville, New York, October, 1961, p. 186.

expression of both children and adults. Thus, a relatively small number of words may constitute a relatively high proportion of the total number used. This important discovery is the key to one of the most qualitative factors that can be identified for spelling. Its value is revealed by findings such as the following:

1. The 100 most frequently used words constitute approximately 60 percent of all normal usage.
2. The 500 most frequently used words constitute approximately 82 percent of all normal usage.
3. The 1000 most frequently used words constitute approximately 90 percent of all normal usage, and
4. The 2000 most frequently used words comprise about 95 percent of all normal usage.[3]

Beyond the first two thousand words, usage tends to be influenced by special vocabularies having to do with particular vocations or areas of special interest, and the thread of commonality tends to disappear. Thus, a total of three thousand words increases the percentage to only 97.66 and 4000 raises it to only 98.73.

There are two major implications for the spelling program in the evidence derived from the word studies. One is that up to the point of two thousand words the school is dealing with a type of content which has considerable importance for every child in the school; beyond that point one is moving into a zone where individualization of the content seems more desirable and necessary. Thus, the first two thousand words comprise what may logically be regarded as the basic or core content of the program. It is by no means the total content of the curriculum in spelling but it is certainly an excellent start.

Although almost all elementary schools use spelling texts, it is difficult to see why texts should be necessary. A school needs to know which words are more frequently used and therefore more basic. But this information is readily available from several studies and could easily be provided in the form of a list at considerable savings to the schools. A teacher who is not sufficiently prepared to teach an elementary core vocabulary without the aid of a book surely is not qualified to be in the classroom. Furthermore, the book

[3] Ernest Horn, *A Basic Writing Vocabulary*, University of Iowa, Monograph No. 4, Iowa City, 1926.

may actually be a hindrance in two significant ways. It mixes and confuses the basic words with those that are less basic, and it tends to introduce a rigidity into the sequence and presentation of the words that is absurd and even detrimental. A wise teacher with a basic list of assigned words can weave them into the curriculum as they are needed and used in the natural course of events. Each word can be checked off as it is mastered so that there is a record of what has been done, and the haphazard aspect of incidental teaching is removed. Some of the modern schools have approached the job of teaching basic spelling words in this way, for it is systematic in addition to being a more natural and meaningful approach. Regardless of whether the words are presented in a manner that is natural or contrived, the school should identify and stress a basic core of words. The core spelling vocabulary pays a handsome 95 percent return and is one of the important characteristics of an excellent program.

Spelling's Giant Booster Mechanism

It seems reasonable to assume that if the elementary school could achieve the teaching of 2000 words comprising 95 percent of normal usage this would be very desirable indeed. Elementary schools, however, can do better than this.

Dolch in an excellent pamphlet on the modern teaching of spelling has identified the chief issue in spelling as the "list versus the learner" approach.[4] In his discussion of the issue he points out a very important matter of which many people seem unaware. Whereas 2000 words can and do provide for a substantial *percentage* of words used by an individual, the number necessary to meet what he calls one's "life spelling needs" is nearer to 10,000 words. Obviously, the elementary school cannot specifically teach 10,000 words—such a task would be physically and mentally impossible. What then should be done?

What seems to be needed is some sort of giant booster mechanism. The step from 2000 to 10,000 words is a phenomenal one and requires some kind of an auxiliary device. The booster is to be found in a change of lens. The school must shift the focus from the

[4] Edward W. Dolch, *The Modern Teaching of Spelling*, Champaign, Illinois, The Garrard Press, 1950.

spelling content itself to the child. It must face up to the fact that teaching the words assigned to any given grade level is for each teacher involved the lesser part of the task. More important is to help each child develop and perfect a way in which he can master new words. This is the power factor which makes it possible for the child to reach out independently on his own and take up where the school program left off.

The Dolch pamphlet contains some excellent suggestions on this matter. It identifies five approaches to the learning of spelling which are described in lay rather than technical terms. Briefly interpreted, lip spelling is a mere habit of the speaking apparatus and is an inferior way of learning to spell. Eye spelling stresses visualization of the word in the "mind's eye"; it is probably the method most widely used in the schools and may be particularly helpful with the common words or with words that are somewhat unusual or tricky. Ear spelling means spelling by sounds, and is more helpful in spelling some of the longer words like Mississippi which tend to be spelled more like they sound. Ear spelling, in contrast to eye spelling, is not very valuable for the common words since they are often the most unphonetic of the language. Hand spelling is exemplified by the child who actually moves his finger over letters to trace the physical outline of the word, and is ordinarily used only in cases where other methods do not seem to get results. Thought spelling has reference to developing the habits of the good speller and is regarded by Dolch as the best solution to poor spelling no matter what the cause. It involves asking—and answering—three important questions:

1. What is the correct pronunciation?
2. Does the sound tell the spelling?
3. How can I remember the hard part?

The word subtle provides an example of this technique. Having established the correct pronunciation, and having determined that the sound does not reveal the correct spelling, one comes to the question of how to remember the hard part. One college student pointed out that sub comes from the Latin, meaning under, and that subtle has an underhanded sort of connotation. This association helped him to establish in his mind the pattern of the spelling.

Presumably, in a technique of this kind a pupil links the idea to be learned with one or more ideas that are already learned. It is what the psychologist would call an association technique. Thus, the spelling of principal is remembered by thinking of the principal as a "pal." An association technique would seem to place some tax on the imagination and power of thinking of a pupil in order to make the necessary links. This, however, could be construed as being beneficial in the sense that it forces the learning to be a more thoughtful process.

The point is that each child needs to be helped to develop a way that is effective for him. It seems advisable to give primary emphasis to the thought method, and to add to that whatever additional elements from the sensory approaches are helpful in creating a smooth working attack for each child. It is worth whatever time it takes to accomplish this. The child who perfects an approach, or combination of approaches, that enables him to unlock or master new words, is well on his way to a higher level of independence, which is the only reasoned hope for attaining mastery of the 10,000 words necessary to meet his life's spelling needs. This factor of independence in attack is spelling's giant booster mechanism.

Spelling's Enrichment Content

Teacher Joe Jones (a fictitious name) taught in a school which was rather conservative in its approach and required its teachers to focus each week on the prescribed words. This prescribed words approach is one of the rituals in spelling held in high regard by school personnel in general. It results in teaching the word icicle in May and the word spring in the fall, but what it lacks in imagination it makes up in its dogged pursuit of the problem.

Joe did what his school required and faithfully taught his prescribed list each week. He added, however, an additional ingredient. Each week on the day of the final spelling he gave five extra words selected from the content of the week's on-going activities. Students did not know in advance what the five words were going to be; they knew only that the words would be selected from units or content that were currently being studied.

The five special words were called bonus words. No pupil was required to try any of them. If a student wished to try any or all of them, however, it was his privilege to do so. A student who missed one of the words in the official list, but tried and successfully spelled one of the bonus words, could still get one-hundred in spelling. He could even miss five of his regular words and get one-hundred if he correctly spelled all of the bonus words. What Joe did was to add a little zest to his spelling, and give it at least some semblance of being in consonance with the rest of the program.

A variation of Joe's plan is similar but somewhat more structured. In this approach the teacher systematically each week works cooperatively with children to point up some of the key or basic words that are a part of what is currently being studied. They may select words such as density, peninsula, and numerator from science, geography, and mathematics because of their frequency and importance in the week's work. These words are posted in some prominent place in the room and supplemented throughout the week with more words as they come into use. By the time of the final spelling such a list might contain 40 or 50 carefully selected words. The students know that their five bonus words will be from this more restricted list, and their study is therefore somewhat more defined. The same mechanics on scoring would prevail.

Such a plan adds a tremendous element of enrichment to the spelling portion of the curriculum. So many good spellers are bored and unchallenged by the weekly list in the text which they already know how to spell. This beefs up the curriculum for them. Curiously enough, it seems also to have a wholesome effect on the less able as well. This is one of the fascinating elements in teaching. Occasionally, a technique or device which is developed for the more gifted turns out to be effective for all concerned and everyone seems to benefit. The enrichment factor in spelling is a valuable qualitative boost.

Personally Appropriated Spelling

In addition to the core content of spelling and the surrounding layer of enrichment content, there is a personal content which provides an individualization ingredient in the program. This individualization ingredient may dip into the core or enrichment material, or go considerably beneath or beyond it in terms of the maturity of the pupil. The following example illustrates one such approach and at the same time weaves it appropriately into the total language arts program.

A primary teacher took her children to the top of a small hill overlooking the village to prime them for a creative writing lesson. The lazy little community stretched out along a forked stream and was very picturesque. The children had never seen their village "from the top side" before and were impressed by the difference in the view. Later, they returned to the classroom to write about what they had seen. At this point their teacher used a rather novel mechanical procedure.

On the board she had written each letter of the alphabet in both small and capital letters. When a child asked how to spell a word he wished to use in his writing she freely supplied it for him and wrote it on the board under the correct letter. For instance if a child asked for the spelling of "beautiful" she wrote it for him on the board under the letter "b." She freely supplied the spellings because she felt that if she did not the child might substitute a word like pretty which he could spell instead of looking up the word he wanted in the dictionary. The net result of such substitutions would be to impoverish and detract from the quality of the writing.

Having asked and received help the child would then record that particular word in his Personalized Dictionary. This dictionary was kept by the child and contained two pages for each letter of the alphabet. It was neatly stapled together, and had an attractive cover which each child had designed and made for himself. The dictionary hung from his desk by a colored string so that it was always readily accessible. Words were added to the dictionaries throughout the year.

The value of such a procedure is that it adds to the spelling content of the curriculum an element that is individualized and personal. It is unlikely that the lists of any two children in a room would be the same. This is in sharp contrast to the core list which is exactly alike for everyone. Both types of content however are vital. One provides a big boost forward on the common words everyone needs to know; the other helps a child come closer to reaching his own life spelling needs. The excellent program in spelling is not complete without such personally appropriated content.

Spelling's Secret Weapon

In 1947 Thomas Horn reported his study on the effect of the corrected test.[5] One group in the experiment followed a weekly plan that is typical of many traditional classrooms. Such a plan involves introduction of the words, attention to pronunciation, formal study, pretest, and final test at the end of the week. An experimental group followed a quite different procedure. This group simply took a test over words which they had not studied, corrected their own papers, studied any errors they had made, and then repeated the same test. The purpose of the study was to determine the effect of allowing children to grade their own spelling.

The results were startling. The experimental group achieved almost as much as the group which formally studied spelling throughout the week. When attention to pronunciation was added to the experimental approach, achievement was approximately 95 percent of the achievement of the group using the traditional plan. Horn concluded that allowing children to correct their own papers was the most important single factor contributing to achievement in spelling. Although the study was conducted with students in the sixth grade, primary teachers who have tried it have reported excellent results even with children in the first grade.

There are several significant aspects to this unusual study. One is simply that it constitutes one of those rare innovations in which the teacher works less and the children learn more. Most teaching ideas seem always to result in extra time and effort on the part of the teacher. It is probably true that most conscientious teachers spend too much time grading papers for children at considerable expense in terms of their own personal lives. Too much of this can drain their vitality and thereby rob them of the greatest gift they can take to a classroom. The self-corrected test technique offers a sort of respite. One might even conclude that the teacher who corrects

[5] Thomas D. Horn, "The Effect of the Corrected Test on Learning to Spell," *Elementary School Journal*, 47 (January, 1947), 277–285.

the papers himself is actually denying children a rich learning opportunity.

A second significant aspect has to do with cheating. Probably a great deal of the cheating which is done in spelling is generated by the pressure children feel to get one-hundred. This approach would seem to remove the incentive to cheat for the purpose is so completely different. The test is used as *a way to learn*. It does not carry the usual warhead. It does, however, carry a bigger payload in that it is a more wholesome and more hygienic approach. The ultraconservative teacher who might hold the fear that "things would get out of hand" can weave in a periodic review lesson in which he grades the papers himself as a precautionary measure and as a check. The self-corrected session itself, however, should be carefully preserved as a way to learn.

There is a third significant aspect of this approach which is difficult to put into words. It is that the spirit of the approach seems to reflect learning in its finest sense—a sort of reaching out process instead of a pouring in. Learning is freed from its usual adult restrictions and becomes more self-active and alive. This quality, unlike any other, lies so much at the heart of a qualitative learning environment.

The Foniks Faktor

One belief held by many professional educators is that, although phonics tends to receive emphasis in connection with learning to read, it may actually be more valuable in learning to spell. Several years ago a simple but interesting innovation along this line was carried out with sixth graders in an Indiana school. The class was divided into two groups which were made as equal as possible in terms of intelligence and achievement in spelling. One group remained in the room with the classroom teacher and continued their regular weekly list approach to spelling. The other group, with a graduate student as teacher, moved to another room for a special approach. The approach of the second group was as follows.

The teacher suggested that they pretend to be Martians and proceeded to teach some Martian words. Martian words were such that their spelling was identical with their sound. Thus, the teacher presented to the class the Martian word for shield which was shagbom. He would pronounce the word for the group and ask how it should be spelled. Several likely spellings would be suggested such as shagbaum, shagbomb, or shagbom. These possible spellings would then be written on the board and discussed, with the intent being to choose the spelling which the class regarded as the most plausible. A vocabulary of twenty words was presented.

In addition, the teacher of the experimental group would frequently request the students to open any of their texts to a specific page, and would give them 3 minutes to study every word on the page. Then he would give them a five word test over the words on that page of material. Three of the five words would be selected because their spelling closely resembled their sound. One of the five words would be selected because its spelling was somewhat like its sound. The fifth word would be chosen because its spelling was unlike its sound. This 3–1–1 distribution was used because it corresponded to the experimenter's preliminary word count and his judgment as to the proportion of the phonic and nonphonic spelling of a running list of words.

The "Martian" experiment ran for a period of fifteen days. A standardized test was given to the entire class before and after the experiment. The test results indicated a clear gain of the phonics group over the control group in thirteen out of fifteen cases. Whether or not this was due to the phonics aspect of the experiment or the novelty aspect is, of course, not known.

The most noted trend in reading emphasis throughout the country seems to be the shift toward larger doses of phonics earlier in the program. If the hunch of educators is correct about the value of phonics to spelling, there should be increasing evidence of that value as a by-product of the altered emphasis of reading instruction. One set of widely used phonetic materials teaches 82 phonetic principles in the first grade alone. Such a massive dose of phonics will surely affect spelling in one way or another. Preliminary findings do seem to indicate superior spelling from the groups emphasizing larger doses of phonics. The Arizona State University experiment, at the end of the first year, did in fact indicate more of an influence on spelling than on reading.[6] On the spelling of phonetic words, the phonics group of children made a median number

[6] Unpublished study by Campus Laboratory School of Arizona State University, Tempe, Arizona, 1960–1961.

of errors of only 1.75 in comparison to the control group which made a median number of errors of 18.75. On the spelling of random words selected from the readers, the median number of errors made by the phonics group was 3.1 compared to 7.1 for the control group. The best evidence available at the present time seems to indicate that an intelligently balanced use of phonics instruction in spelling is a qualitative factor at least in the beginning grades.

The obstacles to applying phonetic generalizations to spelling are formidable and should not be underestimated. About one-half of the words in a dictionary contain silent letters, one-third of the words have more than one acceptable pronunciation, and about one-sixth contain double letters, although only one may be pronounced. It is doubtful that the kind and amount of phonics instruction which would be most beneficial to spelling is as yet known. Nevertheless, there seems to be enough evidence accumulating from teacher reaction and research to indicate that the teaching of sound to letter relationships is a positive element in learning to spell, and a potentially powerful adjunct to the program.

The Levels Arrangement

The arrangement of the curriculum in spelling is not a settled matter. A study by Betts indicated that the agreement in content is considerably less than one would imagine. The study examined eight different text series published since 1940 to determine how many of the words were taught in common by each of the series. The agreement was less than seven percent.[7]

An earlier study by Betts, however, came up with an even more startling factor. This study checked seventeen different text series to determine their agreement with one another with respect to grade placement of the words. The total number of words involved in all the texts ran up to 8,695, but out of this total only one word was placed at the same grade level in each of the series.[8] This finding is almost completely contrary to personal beliefs on the matter, for by and large, teachers and parents show an exaggerated respect for the text which is not warranted by the facts.

[7] A. E. Betts, *Second Vocabulary Grade Placement of Words in Eight Recent Studies*, New York, American Book Company, 1949.

[8] Betts, *Spelling Vocabulary Study. Grade Placement of Words in Seventeen Spellers*, New York, American Book Company, 1940.

Hildreth has suggested what seems to be a very sensible and unique arrangement of the words into six frequency levels. The first level comprises 252 of the most frequently used words. The second level contains 372 of the next most frequently used words. In successive steps the additional levels move out to embrace 457 words in the third level, 462 more in the fourth level, 481 in the fifth, and 962 in the sixth. The total number of words represented in the six levels is 2,986.[9]

In the past, orderly sequence has not been regarded as imperative in spelling as it has been in the case of an area of the curriculum such as mathematics. In other words, a child would not be likely to be at any particular disadvantage in fourth grade spelling if he had for some reason missed spelling in the third grade. This condition is due in part to the nature of spelling as well as to the haphazard arrangement of the words. Hildreth's plan would bring a more discernible element of order into the program. A discernible order of some kind is always helpful in the total task of curriculum planning so that at each segment of the enterprise one knows what comes next, and how it is articulated with the total program.

If, in addition to the levels arrangement, the school can be ingenious enough to mesh the words with the linguistic level of the children concerned, the total program should be greatly improved.

Spelling in Context

In 1927 McKee made a study to determine the relative efficiency of column versus context forms in the teaching of spelling.[10] As a result of his investigation, he concluded that the teaching of spelling in context was less efficient and was an impractical procedure. More recently, Horn has stated in the N.E.A. pamphlet in spelling that:

Research has consistently shown that it is more efficient to study words in lists than in context. Words studied in lists are learned more quickly, remembered longer, and transferred more readily to new context.[11]

[9] Gertrude Hildreth, *Teaching Spelling*, New York, Holt, Rinehart & Winston, 1955.
[10] Paul McKee, "Teaching Spelling by Column and Context Forms," *Journal of Educational Research*, 15 (April, 1927), 246-255.
[11] Ernest Horn, *Teaching Spelling*, Washington, D.C., National Education Association, 1954, p. 16.

Such a statement may be true in a highly specific sense, but seems questionable in a much larger sense. The element of truth in the assertion is that naturally one learns to spell a given word more efficiently by studying that specific word rather than a more loosely arranged target. Thus, the word should be temporarily isolated for a sharp close look and attempted mastery. Spelling it correctly in a list after this good hard look, however, *is not a test of mastery.* Life, fortunately, is such that one does not go around spelling words in lists. Spelling is, instead, a completely functional part of the process of expressing a thought. Words are used in context in the expression of a thought and are properly tested in the same manner. Anything short of this constitutes an inadequate evaluation of the child's mastery of the words.

The point becomes more significant when observations are made of the occasions in which children spell a word correctly in their weekly list, but misspell the same word on other occasions when they are expressing ideas in written form. The classic example of this was the child who was required to practice the word "written" fifty times before going home. He did so and correctly wrote the word. He then penned the following note to his teacher:

I have writen the word fifty times and gone home.

It is not known to what extent words spelled correctly in lists are later spelled incorrectly in context. Teachers can provide an extra boost or reinforcement, however, by dictating the words in sentences or complete paragraphs in order to appraise mastery in more realistic terms. Spelling words today are ordinarily introduced in context as a regular classroom procedure, and this is a sound and logical practice. They should be checked for mastery in the same manner.

Manuscript All the Way

Thoughts that are adequately expressed and words that are correctly spelled deserve a handwriting which pleases the eye. Above all the writing should be legible, and legibility is the logical goal. This is a sensible and wholesome change from the writing of an earlier day which was characterized by flourish and affectation. Although the handwriting of the past was an inextricable part of its own life and times, it does not serve the purposes of the present. The writing sought in the schools today is more simple, more clean-cut, and more crisply a part of today and tomorrow.

The type of handwriting which best serves present purposes is manuscript. Manuscript is superior to cursive writing on practically every count. It is easier for children to learn in their initial writing, for the simplicity of the circles and strokes is more compatible with their degree of motor control and can be learned with less strain. In addition, the child needs to learn only a single letter form of the alphabet for both reading and writing since manuscript closely resembles the print he is beginning to read. The above reasons are largely responsible for the fact that almost all schools begin writing by teaching manuscript. The decision is a sound one.

The mistake made by schools is in shifting to cursive writing in the later grades. Some make the transition in the second grade but most of them change sometime during the third grade. It is an error in judgment to change at all, for it involves shifting from a superior to an inferior style. Many schools will privately admit this, but claim that the parents insist on the change. Parents, for instance, are reported as believing that manuscript is "baby writing." This attitude is completely unfounded, for architects, surveyors, and engineers all use manuscript writing. If parents actually have the attitude that is attributed to them, they are simply not well informed about what is going on in the world.

Occasionally, the reason given for changing to cursive is the need for a legal signature. This is even more preposterous, but indicates the mental level at which many such decisions are made. The author has yet to see a single child of the age of twenty-one regularly enrolled in the elementary school—so the pressure from this source must be at an absolute minimum. Furthermore, if a child did need a legal signature, the one in manuscript is entirely satisfactory. One's habitual signature is his legal signature, whether it is in manuscript or in cursive.

A third reason given for the change is the claim that cursive writing is faster. This claim is probably not even true. Washburne and Morphett demonstrated many years ago that when children used nothing but manuscript on through high school their speed was greater than with cursive.[12] Even if cursive were faster it would

[12] Carlton Washburne and M. V. Morphett, "Manuscript Writing—Some Recent Investigations," *Elementary School Journal*, 37 (1937), 517–529.

not be of any particular importance; for legibility rather than speed is the imperative goal. And where legibility is concerned, manuscript is the undisputed champion. Schools need to reaffirm their leadership on this matter and lead their respective communities. In the qualitative school it is manuscript all the way!

Handwriting's Personal Obligation

The teacher of handwriting has a personal obligation to get the beginner off to the right kind of a start, but this does not mean that a left-hander should be made into a right-hander. In the past, and even today, many left-handed children have been required by their teachers to write with their right hand. This curriculum practice seems completely unjustified.

The human organism is such that the motor activity of the left-handed person is linked with the right hemisphere of the brain. For the right-handed person, the link is with the left hemisphere of the brain. By the time the child enters first grade these patterns are well established. Forcing the child to alter the pattern by writing with his right hand instead of the left creates a disruption in the process. It is not known to what extent this is detrimental. What is known, however, is that if one takes at random one-hundred children who stutter, the group contains an abnormally high incidence of children who have been changed from left-handed to right-handed writing. This does not prove that making such a change causes stuttering; it does, however, flash a danger signal and casts the practice of such changes under a shadow of doubt.

Why is it important enough to take such a chance? Is this particular aspect of individuality somehow out of bounds? Is the world so right-handed that all its inhabitants must be right-handed also? Is the left-handed person at any real disadvantage? It would seem that the burden of proof of any real disadvantage of left-handedness should be placed squarely in the lap of those who advocate the change.

Some of the nation's most prominent authorities on education seem to believe that it is all right for the child to be changed if he is changed early enough and if the transition can be made without strain on the part of the child. This is a most questionable belief.

In the first place, the school does not get the child early enough, his habit associations have already been established. He is oriented to a left-handed existence and is off to a running start. In the second place, who knows whether a child who is being changed is under any strain? It is unrealistic and dangerous to place this much reliance on a teacher's perception, for inner strain may often take place without its outward disclosure. Some children successfully hide it within them.

Left-handedness should be regarded as just another form of rich individuality. It has an attractiveness and grace all its own. Left-handed children who write like cripples with their hand twisted down from the top do so because their teachers were uninformed and placed their paper at a slant that was correct for the right-handed writer but not for the left. There is no reason for the left-handed child to be required to write in such a ludicrous fashion. All the fuss and furor over changing children from left to right should be channeled into more constructive pursuits. The qualitative school allows left-handed children to remain left-handed and it nourishes their handwriting skills in the ways that are most beneficial to them. This is the handwriting teacher's personal obligation to children.

Summary

Considerable importance can be attributed to the development of strength in language tools even though they have come to be regarded as minor aspects of the curriculum. The adequate expression of one's thoughts is further enhanced by correct spelling and legible writing. Of the two tools which are discussed spelling is weighted more heavily because of the higher mental level at which it functions. Reference to handwriting is limited to two factors in which the writer believes serious errors in judgment persist. Ten factors believed to be associated with excellence have been interpreted. Thus, the qualitative program is one which:

1. Gives a priority to the core vocabulary of spelling.
2. Uses spelling's giant booster mechanism.
3. Adds a systematic enrichment content.
4. Weaves in its individualization material.
5. Capitalizes on its secret weapon.

6. Organizes the content by levels.
7. Teaches phonetic generalizations.
8. Evaluates mastery in context.
9. Maintains manuscript throughout the program.
10. Keeps its personal obligation to children.

Chapter 6

Teaching Reading

One August afternoon in Miami a seven year old boy who had completed first grade went over to his old classroom with his former teacher. They were accompanied by another boy who was six and would enter first grade in the fall. In the room, the older boy pulled out one of his pre-primers and proceeded to show the younger child how to read. In a few minutes, the six year old was reading from the second of the pre-primers. The process was something like popping corn. His thrill at his accomplishment was exceeded only by the pride of his parents when he read the book later to them.

Many children learn to read as simply and as easily as the child in Miami. They are the children who are perhaps predestined to read, and would do so even without teachers. Others will learn with the help of intelligent teaching, and for still others the process may become enormously complicated by some creeping psychological paralysis or abnormality. Schools are constantly searching for better ways to facilitate mastery for a greater number of children and to prevent the piling up of disorders on the part of those who experience difficulties.

Parents today do not seem satisfied with the manner in which the schools have performed the task of teaching reading. They realize how important reading is to the personal happiness of their children as well as to their academic success, and they press the schools for quicker and better results. As Cabell Greet expresses it so delightfully in his foreword to Dr. Gray's book:

. . . Isn't there a wonderful modern short cut? Phonemes, semantemes, morphemes, intimes; word counts, meaning counts, nose counts, no-counts. These are new? Surely there is an easier way to teach reading now, even though I can't seem to get my television to work right.[1]

There are a number of interesting experiments and innovations in the teaching of reading, but none of them are short cuts. Each of them requires patience, time, effort, and skillful teaching. And success is rarely due to a single factor; it is more likely to be the result of a constellation of factors. Reading as much as any other aspect of the curriculum reflects the need for a multiple offense and a versatile approach to the problem.

The discussion of qualitative factors in reading takes a slightly different approach than has been used up to this point. Five of the interesting and significant innovations in reading instruction will be presented and interpreted. From these five innovations will be drawn what seems to be some of the conspicuous characteristics of an excellent program.

The ASUCLS Phonics Experiment

One of the more interesting of the experiments with phonics is the one being conducted by the Campus Laboratory School of Arizona State University.[2] The study is a longitudinal one and at the time of writing is not yet completed. Due to the small number of cases involved, the study may never be widely published, yet it is well controlled and the results may be significant.

The study began with the first grade class in the school year of 1960–1961. Twenty-seven children were divided as equally as possible on the basis of intelligence and reading readiness scores. A coin was then flipped to determine which would be the experimental group and which would be the control group. This decision was withheld until after the two groups had been matched in order to eliminate any possible bias. As finally constituted there were fourteen children in one group and thirteen in the other.

The control group followed the basal reading program of one of

[1] William S. Gray, *On Their Own in Reading*, Chicago, Scott, Foresman & Company, 1960.

[2] Unpublished study by Campus Laboratory School of Arizona State University, Tempe, Arizona, 1960–1961.

the large and respected publishers. The program of this publisher includes phonetic analysis but delays teaching the vowel sounds until second grade. The experimental group followed the plan of a prominent publisher of phonetic materials. This program emphasizes a concentrated dose of phonetic analysis and begins with instruction in the vowels. The experimental group moved into the basal reader materials after a period of concentrated work in phonics. The groups, therefore, differed markedly from each other in the degree of emphasis on phonetic analysis.

Each of the groups spent the same amount of time on instruction in reading, and were taught separately so that neither of the groups knew what the other was doing. Each of the groups was assumed also to have the same quality of teaching—one of the more difficult controls—achieved in this study by having the same teacher for both groups. The teacher was an extremely able person and was judged by many observers to be equally enthusiastic and devoted to both groups.

In the spring the children went through a battery of tests. On the Gates test the experimental group achieved higher results on each of the three sections of the test. Their median score on paragraph meaning was 3.1 compared to 2.8 for the control group; on sentence meaning, 3.8 compared to 2.8; and vocabulary, 3.6 compared to 3.1.

On the Metropolitan test the experimental group also outscored the control group on each of the three sections of the test. Their median score on the word picture section was 3.1 compared to 2.7 for the control group; on word recognition, 3.0 compared to 2.5; and on word meaning, 3.5 compared to 2.9.

Differences between the two groups on spelling were even more pronounced. On the spelling of phonetic words the median number of errors made by the control group was 18.75, whereas in the experimental group it was only 1.75. On random words selected from the readers the median number of errors made by the control group was 7.1 compared to 3.1 for the experimental group.

There was an attempt also to check on attitudes toward reading by observation of the number of children from each group who elected to read during their free time. The percentage of children who elected to read in the experimental group was 37.5; for the control group the percentage was 32.1. Attitudes were further checked by providing opportunities for the children to vote on whether or not they would have reading instruction. Forty-five percent of the experimental group voted for reading instruction compared to 24 percent of the control group.

The only part of the evaluation in which the control group exceeded the experimental group was in the number of books read. The median number read by the control group was 13 compared to 7 for the experimental group. In all other aspects of the appraisal the group which had received the more concentrated dose of phonics outscored the other group at the end of the first year of the experiment.

It is significant to note that in this experiment both groups learned to read, and each learned to read very well even though one exceeded the other in terms of the evaluation. It may also be significant that the superiority of the experimental group was more pronounced in spelling than in reading. As the experiment continues it will be of value to know whether the initial superiority persists or tends to be erased as the groups mature.

In a statistical sense the differences in the achievement of the two groups are not significant with respect to reading. They are probably significant in a somewhat larger sense in that at the first grade level any degree of demonstrated superiority is of value to the program. This is because parents attach unusual importance to the ability of their children to read today, and early achievement in reading is culturally as well as academically advantageous to the child. In the case of this particular experiment, children read somewhat better in the experimental group but in addition they *spelled considerably better*, and they *voted to have reading instruction by a ratio of almost two to one over the control group*. All of this seems to add up to a degree of superiority which is of some consequence. Moreover, there is an additional dividend which should not be overlooked: the matter of early independence in reading. Groups which learn enough phonics to attack unfamiliar words reach the goal of independent reading more rapidly than groups in which sound to letter relationship is a somewhat casual part of the program. In these times such an achievement may be of considerable importance.

The Madison Experiment

The practice of having three reading groups has been rather widely accepted in primary classes throughout the entire nation. This is a genuine effort to individualize the program, and although it has meant extra effort on the part of the teacher, it seems to have been carried on willingly and even devotedly. The primary teachers may teach other parts of the program such as mathematics in the form of total group instruction, but they will almost always maintain their three reading groups. It is only in very recent times that the practice has come under rather critical appraisal.

In the school year of 1955–1956 one of the first grade teachers in the Madison Schools challenged the practice. She introduced her single reading lesson in the basic text each day to the entire class. Inasmuch as she was introducing one lesson instead of the usual three, she felt that she could afford to spend more time on it and do it more thoroughly. Following the presentation and work on the basic lesson, all of the children who had mastered the lesson moved into more challenging material. Those who had experienced difficulty with some portion of the lesson were grouped according to the nature of the difficulty. Whatever difficulties had occurred were resolved the same day in order to prevent the piling up of problems. Thus, the *post-lesson groupings were transitory serving a specific purpose and being dissolved upon the achievement of that purpose.* On the following day all of the children would be back together again in large group instruction for the introduction and work on their next basic lesson.

The achievement of the class left little to be desired. Every one of the children learned to read, and in fact the lowest score in the class was 2.8, which was a year above the norm expected for the group as a whole. The highest scores hit 3.9 which was as high as the test measured, and the average for the class as a whole was 3.6. The results were so good that Madison decided to try out the same system next year with the remaining first grades of the school.

Five teachers participated in the plan the following year, and the results again were phenomenal. Of the 131 children tested at the end of this year, every one of the children learned to read, and not a single score fell below the expected norm of 1.8. The average of the entire group was 2.6, and the high again was 3.9. The results were in startling contrast to the preceding year when 45 percent of all the second graders were reading below grade level. In addition to the absence of failing scores under the new plan there was, even more significantly, a higher incidence of top scores than the school had ever achieved before.

What factor (or factors) was responsible for the marked improvement in reading achievement in this school? Madison does not attempt to identify a single factor as causing the change, but attributes a large share of the improvement to the shift in grouping procedures, for other aspects of the program were relatively unchanged. How could a simple change of this nature be so momentous?

The use of three reading groups involves a certain degree of *status*. It is good to be in the top group and uncomfortable to be in the bottom one. To be in the bottom group is something like being consigned to Lower Slobbovia, and children seem to know which group they are in, regardless of how carefully the teachers attempt to conceal it. The difficulty is compounded by the fact that as the year progresses the low group gets farther and farther behind, with the children becoming more and more discouraged. Thus, children who come bounding to school in September with positive attitudes toward school become disenchanted as the year unfolds. They develop a distaste for reading and may even dislike school in general.

To some, the above reasoning may seem far-fetched. Psychology, however, in recent times has become increasingly aware of the significance of the self-concept. It may well be that no aspect of child rearing is more vital than helping a child to grow up with the feeling that he is a worthy self. The three-group approach to reading is tampering with the self-concept in a manner which may be detrimental to a substantial segment of the class. The Madison plan overcomes this psychological hazard. It keeps all the children on the steady road to progress by teaching sequential basic lessons systematically to the entire group, but does so without the usual accompanying lock-step which slows down more able children. Thus, not only were more children successful than ever before in learning to read, but more children than ever scored at the top of the test.

Many people misunderstand the Madison plan; they feel that it is a plan which does away with individualization and groups. In no sense of the word does it do this; *in fact the plan actually results in more individualization and groups.* There is an important difference, however, in the character of the groups, for they are less fixed. They serve their purpose and are then dissolved. Each group lasts only a day, and the child knows that tomorrow he will be right back in the mainstream of events with the rest of the class. Thus, the plan emphasized individualization *with protection of the self-concept.*

The New Castle Reading Experiment

One of the very successful innovations in the teaching of reading was conducted by Glenn McCracken in the Thaddeus Stevens School at New Castle, Pennsylvania.[3] The purpose of this experiment was to evaluate the effectiveness of teaching reading by an enlarged film image on a screen, using the textbook only for testing and practice. The filmstrips were designed to parallel the text, and every lesson was introduced and taught to the entire class from the image projected on the screen. Thus, the children could all get the same kind of initial introduction, and could later discuss together the projected material. After working together in this fashion, the class would turn to their individual texts for practice and completion of the lesson.

Three sections of the first grade tried out the plan during the school year of 1949–1950. At the end of the year they were given the Gates Reading Test and made median scores of 2.45, 2.72, and 2.70. The lowest score made was 1.99 so there were, in fact, no low scores in the entire group. The experimental program was continued in the first grades in the school year of 1950–1951 and also in 1951–1952, with comparable results in terms of reading achievement. The achievement of the three grades during the experimental years was better than any of the previous classes of the same grade level as far back as the school records showed.

The before and after comparison of the experiment is one of the

[3] Glenn McCracken, "The New Castle Reading Experiment: A Terminal Report," *Elementary English,* 30 (January, 1953), 13–21.

very impressive aspects of the project. Before the experiment, Thaddeus Stevens School had usually ranked about 27th out of the 28 schools in New Castle. During the experiment it jumped to 1st and 2nd place in the city. The year following the experiment, the first grade classes again fell near the bottom of the city ranking. Here again is an approach which is somewhat off the beaten path of reading instruction, yet seems to yield excellent results. What is the qualitative ingredient in this particular approach?

Like the Madison plan the New Castle experiment introduced a single basic lesson to the entire group. Inasmuch as it was a film lesson type of introduction, it was probably more carefully prepared than what most teachers are able to do on a sustained day-by-day basis. Children apparently moved along together on the basic lessons, so that the self-concept may be assumed to have been protected in the New Castle plan also. The chief feature of the plan in addition to those common aspects seems to be the systematic exploitation of a visual method. Apparently, there was a high degree of motivation and interest in the film strip approach. By the time children moved into the text material itself they were at a high level of motivation to complete the lesson.

Although the achievement at Stevens was not as high as that at Madison it is in one sense more significant, as many of the children at Stevens were from millworker families who spoke a foreign language at home. At Madison, however, this factor was not involved, the children being from a relatively higher socio-economic group. Perhaps this is a key to one of the intrinsic strengths of the New Castle plan. It took students from a school that had more or less consistently ranked at the bottom of the list in reading achievement, and brought them up to the top of the distribution. It is generally acknowledged that a rich background of experience is an invaluable aid to a child in learning to read. Where children come to school with a somewhat impoverished experiential background, the school must attempt in some manner to enrich it. Perhaps the New Castle plan *hastens the pace of this process,* and lessens the gap without resorting to the more usual extension of the readiness period. In fact, it may well be that the plan contains a built-in readiness of its own, which allows the children to go right on with their more favored colleagues without ever having to experience the stigma and psychological waste of being held back. The plan seems to demonstrate that there is a way of successfully teaching children with less favored backgrounds how to read, and that the extended readiness programs of some schools may be less necessary than is generally believed.

Individualized Reading

Individualized reading is one of the refreshing innovations that has moved into current practices. Teachers have always attempted to have some degree of individualization in their program, but the approach which is going by the name of individualized reading represents a bolder and more clear-cut break with traditional methods. One of the conspicuous requirements for success of the method seems to be a belief on the part of the teacher in the importance of developing in children a larger measure of personal responsibility for their own success in reading. The teacher who has this personal conviction regarding the importance of self-direction seems more oriented to the kind of organization and detail that is essential for making the program a success.

Pupils should be developed to the point where they can read and work independently for short periods without constant supervision, in order for the program to be put into effect. The procedures have been used effectively with children having a range of reading ability extending from low second grade level up to and including an adult level. The program is summarized as follows:

1. A large number of suitable books is assembled. This would ordinarily include sets of eight or ten copies of several different basal readers, as well as fiction, travel, history, biography, science, and poetry. The range of this material must at any given time extend from what the lowest reader in the class can read *independently* on up to the appropriate level of difficulty for the best readers in the group.

2. The children must be functionally oriented to the new procedures. This means that they must be taught how to select books for themselves, how to get the book which they have read properly checked, and how to record the book if their mastery of it has been

checked out as satisfactory. In addition, the children must understand the importance of their own efforts to the success of the program.

3. After orientation and the beginning of the program, the child keeps in his possession at all times a book of his own choice. As he reads he keeps a vocabulary list of the words which cause him difficulty in his independent reading.

4. The teacher will have a conference with each child at least once a week. The conference lasts from three to ten minutes, and provides an opportunity for the teacher to check on strengths and weaknesses. Any specific problems which are observed are recorded and become a basis for further reading instruction.

5. Reading instruction parallels the other aspect of the program, and is generally handled in small groups. This instruction systematically builds reading skills so that nothing is left to chance.

6. Children who have read the same book may meet with one another in small groups to discuss it, and may share what they have read with the entire class. This avoids the false audience situation which exists when a child reads to other children all of whom have the same book.

7. In order to avoid a bottleneck resulting from the necessity for the teacher to personally check each book, the system makes use of pupil checkers. The first child to complete a book is checked by the teacher and becomes the pupil checker of that book. The name of the pupil checker is recorded in the book file.

The individualized reading program seems to break the lock-step method of instruction in which all children are more or less compelled to move along in the same material at the same rate. Judging by the amount of reading done, it promotes more extensive and varied reading. Attitudes toward reading are more favorable, for choosing what one wants to read is not only more fun, but reduces tension and anxiety to a minimum. The personal responsibility a child has for his own success is a distinctive contribution to the development of maturity and self-direction. All in all, this innovation looks definitely promising. It seems to be qualitative with respect to the degree of individualization which it achieves, as well as to its successful involvement of children in the assumption of more responsibility for their own progress.

Reading Based on Creative Writing

Individualized as the preceding program is, there is one which is even more so; it is the San Diego County plan of initiating reading through creative writing.[4] In a way it is the logical extension of the experiments with individualized approaches, but it is bolder, more exciting, and more creative.

In his interpretation of the plan Van Allen sets the tone and almost states the rationale by the following quotation from Gibran:

> The teacher who walks in the shadow of the temple among his followers, gives not of his wisdom but rather of his faith and his lovingness.
>
> If he is indeed wise he does not bid you enter the house of his wisdom, but rather leads you to the threshold of your own mind.[5]

As one might infer from this passage of Gibran's, the plan makes more use of the experience the child brings to school when he comes, and attempts to build upon this for the content of the reading program.

The plan began in the 1956 preschool workshop when several first grade teachers decided to put into practice what they had been saying for several years about giving children a maximum opportunity for language development. Their experiences with children's creative writing had convinced them that children have within themselves the basic material for a program with ceilings unlimited.

How to begin such a program was the big question. The use of prepared readiness sheets was out because they did not represent the ideas of the children to be taught. It did not seem appropriate to the teachers to begin with a list of basic sight words because they might not be the words which reflected the thinking and interests of the children during the early days of first grade. Furthermore, they couldn't even begin with group stories dictated by the children because only a few participated at first and they wanted participation on the part of every child from the very beginning.

[4] R. Van Allen, "Initiating Reading Through Creative Writing," *Twenty-Second Yearbook of the Claremont College Reading Conference*, Claremont, California, 1957, pp. 109–116.

[5] Khalil Gibran, *The Prophet*, New York, Alfred A. Knopf, 1923, p. 56.

Thus, there was a genuine effort to make it an experience approach, and they decided to try using children's earliest self-expression in writing as a point of departure. They reasoned that when a child makes a picture he is expressing an idea which has meaning to him, and to him it is a way *of really writing.* Putting what he is saying with his picture into words would be the beginning of his reading. Thus, each day the teachers would give each child repeated opportunities *to come to the threshold of reading without forcing an entrance.*

In each classroom children were asked to bring a picture of their own choosing to the "reading group." There the teacher invited comment about each picture, and together, she and the child decided on a story to be written on the picture. The rest of the children watched eagerly as they saw the speech of one child take form on his picture. They participated by helping the teacher decide about initial sounds, capital letters, and punctuation.

Reading the story which had been written was not a requirement, but the teachers found that each succeeding day, additional children would try to step across the threshold by reading something which they had said for their picture story.

The children's pride and interest in their stories was so great that with the help of the teachers they were bound into books for the reading table. Every child had a desire to read them because they were what he and his classmates had written. The vocabulary used was found to be three to four times as great as that used in any standard series of pre-primers. The children who wrote and read from their own experiences prior to reading from basic readers could then read the textbooks with ease, and were able to read from fifteen to twenty pre-primers in a matter of a month.

The report further indicated that the elements of phonics which were learned in the letter-by-letter recording of language in writing were used in a functional situation in reading. The teacher always made sure that the minimum phonics program of the basic reading series had been accomplished by every child. Thus, a maximum reading opportunity, developed naturally from children's experiences, was combined with elements of systematic instruction to the mutual advantage of each child.

It would be difficult to develop a more individualized method of teaching initial reading than the San Diego County approach. It shatters the rigid routines that flourish in so many of the nation's primary classrooms and opens the door to a program that is limited only by the language and experience level of the children concerned. It deliberately avoids the use of predetermined, preplanned materials in its beginning stages, for it reflects a basic conviction that *no preplanned materials developed by specialists can equal the resources that exist within the children themselves.* As in the case of the social studies factor of using the classroom itself as a laboratory for social living, this method contains its own intrinsic or built-in motivation. The plan reflects a dynamic sort of faith in the individual and a heartening demonstration of creative teaching as well. Hats off to San Diego County for what seems to be an excellent example of a creative approach to the teaching of reading.

A Basic Element

The five experiments and innovations presented moved in something of a progression from specificity to latitude. Thus, the ASUCLS experiment with phonics, the Madison plan with post-lesson individualized grouping, and the New Castle plan with pre-lesson visual motivation all utilized basal readers and followed them rather closely except for the specific variations in procedure that were being studied.

The pattern of instruction known as individualized reading, however, moved away from basal reading plans as such, using the readers in more of an incidental manner. It devoted itself initially to building up a considerable variety of reading matter from the full spectrum of books for children, and attempted to place in the hands of each child a book that was just right for him. Thus, it had more latitude in both materials and procedure than the other plans. It still provided for basic instruction in reading, however, based on the emerging needs of the children concerned.

In the San Diego County experiment of teaching reading through creative writing, there was a still greater movement away from preplanned reading matter, and the materials to be used were creatively developed from the children's own ideas and experiences. This plan reflected the widest latitude, and the greatest individualization of any of the programs, and provided basic elements of reading instruction functionally derived from experiences in writing.

Regardless of the approach to be used in teaching reading, one common element which must be present in a program is some kind of basic instruction in word perception. Word perception is at the heart of the reading process, and involves a multiple set of approaches to word attack all of which need to be developed. None of them can be slighted if the reading of children is to be fully developed.

The one which parents know best and are most concerned with is phonetic analysis. The press throughout much of the nation has conveyed to parents the idea that professional education does not believe in phonics and slights it in the teaching of reading. Actually, all basal reading series have a rather complete program of phonetic analysis built into their programs, and almost all the prominent authorities in reading attach importance to this approach. The difference in point of view concerning phonics is largely a matter of degree. Flesch and many parents who follow him regard phonics as *the method of teaching reading.* Reading authorities on the other hand regard phonics as *one of the aids in word analysis,* and believe it must be accompanied by other approaches if the reading of an individual is to be effective. Thus, Gray points out that the child might successfully sound out "Mi piace leggere," but unless he knows Italian it has no meaning to him.[6]

A second approach to word perception which should be used in conjunction with phonetic analysis is the use of context clues. The word bank sounds the same whether it appears as "money in the bank," "bank the fire," or "bank of the stream." The only way a child can know which way it is intended is by being sensitive to the context in which it is used. The English language is full of this potentiality for various meanings, and so after a word is sounded out, it should then be checked to be sure that it *makes sense.* To the extent that meaning is considered important in reading, the use of context clues is important also. If reading is to be considered as mere word calling, as some seem to regard it, then context clues of course serve no useful purpose.

There are occasions when the meaning cannot be derived even

[6] William S. Gray, *On Their Own in Reading,* Chicago, Scott, Foresman & Company, 1960, p. 12.

with the effective combination of *sounding out plus the use of context*. In the sentence "the seven fluffy signets swam across the lake," a child can correctly sound out the word signet, and he can infer from context that it is some sort of living thing, but he will not know precisely what it is (on his own) without checking it in the dictionary. Thus, use of the dictionary is an additional necessary approach for independence and maturity in reading.

The three approaches above plus configuration (memory of word form), and structural analysis (analysis of the meaning units in a word—root, inflectional endings, prefixes, and suffixes) constitute what reading authorities regard as the necessary aspects of adequate word perception. Parents should be extremely cautious about giving schools the impression that they believe phonetic analysis is all that is required, for in the final analysis they will get precisely what they want. It is difficult to believe that the impression they have registered on this vital matter really represents their considered judgment. But if it is, many schools will revert to an approach which can only result in impoverished instruction. In that event it will not be merely the child who is short changed.

Summary

It seems obvious that children can learn to read successfully by any one of a number of approaches and some can even learn by themselves. It is the purpose of reading instruction, however, to increase the incidence as well as the level of success and the more effective innovations may indicate how this can be done.

One aspect of excellence in a reading program is the degree to which it can relate itself to the experiences children have had before they come to school. This is significant in the sense of establishing a natural transition or induction into the reading process. It is also significant with respect to the development of both sides of the reading coin. For reading is not merely getting meaning from a printed page: reading is also bringing meaning to a printed page. The San Diego plan for teaching reading through creative writing brings into fuller play this neglected aspect of the reading process and uniquely builds upon the children's own ideas and experiences.

A second aspect of excellence has to do with the degree to which the program can enable children to get off to a good initial start and experience success in the undertaking. This is of particular importance today because of the mood of the times. The attitude of parents today toward their children's reading is one which expects quick success and is not tolerant of any delay in the process. Children feel this pressure and may be tremendously affected by it. The intent of professional education on this matter has been to protect children, and build a margin of additional safety for them by extending the readiness period for those who seem to require it. This, however, has not solved the problem for it has run headlong into the demand of the parents for quick success, and may actually have generated additional pressure on children rather than serving as a protective device. One may criticize the validity of parental attitudes on this matter but this in no way resolves the dilemma. The attitude is a reality, and one must deal with what the realities are rather than with what he might wish them to be. This second aspect of excellence is well illustrated by the Madison plan. This approach directed itself at a minimum core of necessary and sequential steps in learning to read. Then it concentrated on *mastery for each child each day on each step in the pattern of basic instruction.* In effect it seemed almost to build a pattern of success. The discouragement associated with being in a lower group and getting farther and farther behind was minimized by the Madison procedures.

A third aspect of excellence relates to the degree to which the program can teach children to read successfully even though they have meager backgrounds. This is significant because the world is full of children with meager backgrounds, and they comprise a substantial segment of the total school population. Every elementary teacher expects a wide diversity of background in her pupils and also expects to have a percentage of children with relatively deprived backgrounds. Some of these children may be from foreign-speaking homes and suffer a language handicap. Others may be from homes lacking in general intellectual stimulation and encouragement. Other things being equal, the excellence of a reading program is reflected in the degree to which it can get the job done in spite of these deprivations. The New Castle Plan was a conspicuous success under precisely such circumstances. Since the chief characteristics of this plan was the use of prepared film materials, it seems likely that increased use of such resources within the formal reading program itself may be particularly promising for children with meager backgrounds.

A fourth aspect of excellence relates to the use of phonics in the initial phases of the reading program. Inasmuch as the control group of the ASUCLS experiment also received instruction in the regular amount of phonics included in the materials of a major publisher, the experiment was not a test of phonics versus non-phonics. The experiment is more accurately designated as a study of the effect of a marked increase of phonics in the first grade. The results of this portion of the experiment indicated that the increase was beneficial to the reading of the experimental group as evidenced by the forms of evaluation used. This is significant in the sense that it bears upon the ability of the child to *read independently* at an earlier stage of the program. Without this sound to letter training he is stopped every time he comes to an unfamiliar word. Children would seem to need enough phonics to be able to logically attack unfamiliar words, and again in view of the powerful affect of parental attitudes it seems desirable that they develop this skill as rapidly as possible. This is true particularly if it can proceed without evidence that it is detrimental to the children in any way. It should be pointed out in this sense that the evidence is not detrimental. The overuse or abuse of any approach can be detrimental to the development of children, and the mood of the times is such that excesses with respect to overuse of phonics will no doubt occur in many communities throughout the country. Qualitative factors in the reading program must be identified, however, in such a manner that this ingredient is kept in balance. With the balance factor clearly in focus it seems reasonable to suggest that independence in reading is promoted by a discernible stress on phonics early in the program, and that this is a qualitative ingredient within the larger approach.

A fifth aspect of excellence is indicated by the degree to which there is advancing maturity in word perception. This is a larger factor than phonics and refers to competency in multiple forms of word attack. The sounding out of words is balanced and strengthened by concomitant use of context clues, structural analysis, skill in using the dictionary, and a quick, smooth assimilation of the image or configuration of a rapidly growing stock of words. These skills are in a sense the muscle of the program. In the highly skilled reader they are as effortlessly invoked and coordinated as the actions of a superb athlete in his chosen endeavor. This maturity, based as it is upon multiple approaches to word mastery, is a balancing factor which protects children against splinter movements and elements of faddishness in current programs. It is a key factor in the appraisal of excellence in any program to be used.

The sixth and last quality to be suggested here is the degree to which a given program can be individualized. The traditional three group approach to reading instruction does not achieve adequate individualization and may even be deterimental in its abuse of the self-concept. This is particularly true when the groups tend to be permanently fixed. The Madison use of post-lesson groupings was an effective approach to individualization and one which remained sensitive to problems of status and the self image. Marked individualization was a characteristic of the approach used by San Diego County, and is the central emphasis of the current innovations which are known as individualized reading programs. Implementation of procedures which realistically relate to and build upon the capacities of the children involved is the sine qua non of a qualitative approach.

It is obvious that an infinite number of factors associated with excellence in reading programs might be identified. Those which have been suggested here aspire to indicate some of the aspects of quality which are more uniquely in consonance with the times. Thus, the excellent program is one which:

1. Utilizes and builds effectively upon the experiences children have had before they come to school.
2. Concentrates on procedures for maximizing the incidence of success during the first year.
3. Provides for the strengthening of meager backgrounds by resources that are built within the program itself.
4. Stresses sufficient phonetic elements to achieve the earliest possible achievement of independent reading.
5. Strives for maturity of word perception through the emphasis of multiple approaches to word attack.
6. Relates any given approach humanely and effectively to the capacities of the children involved.

Chapter 7

Elementary Mathematics

Arithmetic is elementary mathematics and is a product of the mind of man. Many people still regard it as a skill subject rather than a content subject. It is true of course that there are many skills to be acquired in arithmetic, but arithmetic is far more than a collection of skills; it is a system of ideas. The child who masters these ideas is much better prepared to take his place in the world today, for in modern society mathematics underlies all technological development. It is such an indispensable tool of thought that one who does not master it will find himself blocked off from an increasing range of vocational choices.

Of all the curriculum challenges which confront the schools none is more formidable than the task of equipping the next generation of children with the mathematical understanding they need in order to assume an adequate role in their world. The mathematics program is expected to undergo radical changes. Haan interprets those changes as follows:

In the next few years there will be many significant changes in mathematics and in mathematics instruction. The concept of sets, originally developed by Cantor, will dominate mathematics. The separation of geometry, algebra, and analysis will end. Solid geometry will disappear as a separate course. Algebra will be concerned with groups, rings, and fields. Statistical reasoning will be part of mathematics instruction at all levels. Euclidean geometry will give way to three dimensional geometry. Probability and statistical inference will be introduced earlier. At the elementary level all mathematics will be unified, with concepts from the entire field of mathematics taught throughout the grades.[1]

[1] Aubrey Haan, *Elementary Curriculum: Theory and Research*, Boston, Allyn and Bacon, 1961, p. 192.

Obviously, exciting changes are in store for children in the wonderful new world of mathematics, but these changes are still somewhat blurred at the moment, and await the more careful formulation and pilot work of the specialists. In the interim, what kind of a program might constitute a bridge that would help to link the best of the old with the best of what is predicted for the new? The following characteristics written at the arithmetical level of understanding which most teachers understand are submitted as a possible bridge between the old and the new.

Meaning and Self-Discovery

An enlightened primary teacher took a job in a very backward school where children had learned to manipulate numbers without understanding what they were doing. One day she went to the board and wrote the following subtraction problem:

$$
\begin{array}{r}
37 \\
-18 \\
\hline
\end{array}
$$

Out of her thirty children twenty of them could get the correct answer but not a single one of them could explain it. So she walked over to a device known as a place value pocket, and in the tens pocket placed three bundles of popsicle sticks with ten in each bundle. In the units pocket she placed seven individual sticks to represent the seven ones. Then she asked the children if they could prove that their answer was correct. One of the newly enrolled children came up timidly and performed the proof. He took one of the bundles of ten from the tens group, removed the rubber band to transform it into ten additional ones, and demonstrated to the class that the problem involved regrouping three tens and seven ones into two tens and seventeen ones in order to be able to proceed with the subtraction. There are a number of adults in today's society who could not rationalize the problem as clearly as the above child because they learned arithmetic mechanically rather than meaningfully.

Since the early texts on pedagogy teachers have been admonished to teach arithmetic meaningfully, but for many years the problem seemed bogged down in implementation. Today in the better schools there is more sophistication to the movement. More teachers seem to grasp what it is all about, and they seem to be better equipped with the technology for achieving it. Thus an upper grade teacher may distribute three-dimensional cardboard models around his room several days before he plans to take up linear surface area with his class. The students may unfold the models and examine them at their leisure. Many of them will discover for themselves how to compute the area before it is ever brought up in class.

In a seventh grade the writer observed students in the process of discovering the relationship between the diameter and circumference of circles. They were using a device called a Circlometer[2] which consisted of a grooved measuring device and four wooden circles each of which was a different diameter. Placing a handle on the smallest of the circles a student rolled it carefully down the grooved measuring device to determine the circumference. Each circle was measured and the circumference was determined and recorded. Then the students were invited to take their recorded data and generalize: "Is there a definite relationship between the diameter and the circumference of a circle?" The students' efforts roughly approximated 3.14 and they were informed that 3.1416 was considered accurate enough for all practical requirements, although the exact ratio of circumference to diameter is not known. The understanding of students who work through such a process is surely superior to the understanding of students who are allowed merely to memorize a formula.

In recent times the stress upon a meaningful arithmetic has been the dominant theme running through the professional literature. A good start has now been made in the actual implementation of the idea in the classroom, and any changes contemplated for the schools of tomorrow should make every effort to hold and consolidate the gains that have been made. Building into the program additional opportunities for children to understand and discover mathematical principles for themselves is one of the rich veins of curriculum development. It gives a laboratory quality to the program of mathematics. It calls for a higher and more stimulating level of mental activity from teachers and students alike, and it

[2] Distributed by the Winston Company, 1010 Arch Street, Philadelphia 7, Pennsylvania.

promises a more exciting return. Few aspects of the program of elementary mathematics are more indicative of a qualitative approach.

Conceptual and Manipulative Devices

In the past a teacher might have taught a lesson on measures such as pints, quarts, and gallons without having the actual measures in the room for children to see and to handle. A child in such a class may have memorized the units without having any real conception of what the measures were actually like. The enlightened classroom does not make this mistake. It attempts to follow the principle of moving in a sequence from the concrete, to the semi-concrete, to the abstraction. For example, the concept of area in early grades may be introduced by going out and measuring the school garden preliminary to deciding what can be planted. The dimensions of the garden can be reduced to a cardboard model in the classroom where the deliberations are continued. From these experiences the child can be taught the area formula which is an abstraction. A qualitative school regards conceptual devices and materials as an indispensable part of its mathematics program, and systematically builds them up in each room just as it would build up its printed materials.

One of the most versatile and inexpensive of the valuable aids that are used in a modern classroom is the string of one-hundred spools. This device costs practically nothing. It consists of 100 spools on a string or wire, and is placed in the room where it can be easily seen and manipulated by the children. The 13th, 38th, 63rd, and 88th spools are cut in half to concretely portray ⅛, ⅜, ⅝, and ⅞. Additionally, the 34th and 67th spools are cut into thirds to show ⅓ and ⅔. At the primary level this device is useful for simple counting, for crossing the tens as in the example of ten plus three, and for seeing numbers that are less than 100 in relation to the total number of one-hundred. At the middle and upper grades the device is still useful for fractions, decimals, and percents. This simple aid is one of the most versatile the school can provide.

A second interesting type of material is the Stern Structural

Arithmetic materials.[3] Developed by Catherine Stern, the beginning set is used for the last half of kindergarten and the first half of first grade. Inasmuch as they are rather expensive, schools often provide a set to be shared by two or more rooms. The Stern materials strive to achieve all of the properties of abstract numbers. An example of their application and value is indicated by one portion which is called the number frames. These frames resemble a nest of square trays which for convenience in storing fit inside one another. A teacher can take the nine tray and sit down with the children as she might sit down with a small reading group and teach them the story of nine. The story of nine unfolds as the children proceed to fill the nine tray. The nine block just fits into the tray so it is placed in the tray first. Then all the possible combinations of nine are also placed into the tray. When the tray is filled it holds the eight and the one block as well as the one and the eight, the seven and two and the two and seven, the five and four and the four and five, and the six and three along with the three and six. This is the story of nine—learned by the actual manipulation and placement of attractive, scientifically designed materials into all of the possible combinations of nine. When the child has learned the stories of nine, eight, seven, six, five, etc. he has moved a good portion of the way toward mastering his fundamental addition combinations. More important, it has been accomplished through understanding rather than memorization.

A spot check of classrooms in an excellent elementary school indicated that the following conceptual devices were being used in grades one through eight:

1. The Stern Structural Materials.
2. The One-hundred Spools.
3. The Giant Ruler and Thermometer.
4. The Place-Value Pocket.
5. The Abacus.
6. The Fraction Board.
7. Wooden Area Models.
8. Three-dimensional Cardboard Models.

[3] Distributed by Houghton-Mifflin, 777 California Avenue, Palo Alto, California.

9. The Circlometer.
10. The Cuisenaire Rods.[4]

The above materials are typical of what is being used in some of the modern schools. If a mathematics program doesn't have such conceptual devices in active use, it probably has made no substantial effort to build up its *library of concrete aids*. Building them up, refining their use, and making them a vital part of the day-by-day operation is an essential aspect of a qualitative approach.

Functional Arithmetic

Functional arithmetic is the arithmetic that is a normal and natural aspect of the child's existence. A primary teacher writes on the board the following:

On Friday we will have our Valentine party. Six children in our class will bring the cookies for the party. How many cookies should each child bring if there are to be 36 people at the party and each person is to have two cookies apiece?

One child instantly says each child should bring six cookies. He is asked to explain. Another child says, "I think each of them will need to bring twelve cookies." He is invited to explain. A third child says that he agrees the answer is twelve but worked the problem in a different way. He wants to show how he did it. Is this just wheel spinning and wasted time? Isn't the nature of mathematics such that it requires systematic sequential instruction rather than this kind of a haphazard approach?

The arithmetic program does need to be systematic and sequential; almost all the mathematics authorities agree on this point. But arithmetic also needs to be a vital and meaningful part of one's existence. The two ideas are not basically incompatible, although they have been presented as incompatible in some of the earlier discussions of incidental teaching. The hard core of the program is the portion dealing with the basic nucleus of mathematical understanding. It is sequentially and systematically presented, and is generally well done in text or workbook series. What the text or work-

[4] Distributed by Cuisenaire Company of America, Inc., 235 East 50th Street, New York 22, N.Y.

book cannot possibly do, however, is satisfactorily *relate to the experiences of a given classroom.* The experiences of a particular classroom are unique elements which can never be satisfactorily mirrored in commercial materials.

The Valentine incident above supplies a missing ingredient; it draws from the real setting of the situation the opportunities for arithmetic to function in the normal processes of classroom life. This allows mathematics to have a more vital role and provides graphic representation of how and why mathematics is a functional part of one's existence. The mathematics from the book alone cannot do this. There is nothing haphazard about this practice when it is intelligently conducted for it may either either precede or follow through on the sequential aspect which has been or will be developed. It is therefore reinforcing. Additionally, it is one of the primary contributors to the basic intent of creating a meaningful program.

Functional arithmetic involves a minor element of rescheduling. Instead of having a formal period of arithmetic forty minutes a day for five days a week, a teacher might have his time arranged for forty minutes a day three days a week, or thirty minutes a day five days a week. In those periods he moves ahead on his systematic sequential instruction. He has, however, picked up in this manner from fifty to eighty minutes a week which may legitimately be devoted to functional arithmetic as the opportunities arise. He looks for *the teachable moment,* and attempts to develop a sensitivity to natural openings or opportunities. Some teachers do this remarkably well. Under such an arrangement the formal periods are somewhat more streamlined, but this streamlining may be advantageous rather than detrimental. Furthermore, the combination of *formal plus applied mathematics is a much stronger thrust.* This factor is a vital one, and it will continue to be a characteristic of the better programs.

The Function of Diagnosis

There is no area of the curriculum that lends itself more naturally to diagnosis than arithmetic, nor is there an area of the curriculum that can benefit more from its use. The diagnosis does not require that one be a specialist in mathematics, nor does it require elaborate or expensive equipment. In fact, all that it requires is an understanding on the part of the teacher as to precisely what it is he is attempting to teach, plus a recognition of the importance of determining whether or not he is getting the job done. One school tried the following simple, homemade project with the indicated results.

First the school broke down the fundamental operations with whole numbers into the specific *types of problems* that children would encounter. The breakdown into types attempted to provide for a range and variety that would be sufficient to indicate practical mastery of the fundamental operations. Each type was specific, and differed from the others in a sense which could cause it to be a particular source of learning difficulty. After this analysis was prepared, it was organized for the benefit of the experimenters in a very simple form. On one side of a sheet of paper the specific idea or concept involved was stated, and parallel to the idea were illustrative examples. For the fundamental operations, in addition, the analysis was organized as shown on page 96.

The second step was to prepare and administer to the children simple tests which required only a single period for both administering and analysis. The test for addition was on a single sheet and contained an example of each of the specific problem types. The class worked the examples in ten minutes. They traded papers and scored them in another ten minutes. Then the teacher called for a show of hands on each problem type to determine the number of students who had missed each particular problem. In approximately thirty minutes, using homemade devices that could be employed in any school, the teacher had an extremely valuable record of the results. He knew how many misses were made on each type of problem, and what reteaching was necessary in order to achieve mastery. Thus, he was now in a position to exercise economy of teaching-learning time and teach specifically what had not yet been learned. This is careful target shooting rather than a scattered and wasteful use of ammunition.

Six weeks of refined activity of this kind brought the children involved gains of a year and a half as measured by standardized tests. Wisely and skillfully used this is an effective and powerful technique.

Paper and pencil diagnosis of the type just described indicates

Concepts	Examples

1. Bridging the tens.

$$\begin{array}{cc} 7 & 5 \\ +4 & +8 \end{array} \quad 9+3=$$

2. Carrying in one's place.

$$\begin{array}{r} 318 \\ +429 \\ \hline \end{array}$$

3. Carrying in ten's place.

$$\begin{array}{r} 575 \\ +262 \\ \hline \end{array}$$

4. Carrying in hundred's place.

$$\begin{array}{r} 4921 \\ +1577 \\ \hline \end{array}$$

5. Carrying in alternate places.

$$\begin{array}{r} 1819 \\ +4452 \\ \hline \end{array}$$

6. Carrying in consecutive places.

$$\begin{array}{r} 6748 \\ +3277 \\ \hline \end{array}$$

7. Carrying into zero.

$$\begin{array}{r} 5056 \\ +1772 \\ \hline \end{array}$$

8. Power problems.

$$\begin{array}{r} 875679 \\ 999856 \\ 578995 \\ 789696 \\ 562755 \end{array}$$

9. Denominate numbers.
   (no carrying)

$$\begin{array}{r} 7 \text{ lbs. } 3 \text{ ozs.} \\ +5 \text{ lbs. } 5 \text{ oz.} \\ \hline \end{array}$$

10. Denominate numbers.
    (with carrying)

$$\begin{array}{r} 5 \text{ lbs. } 9 \text{ ozs.} \\ +2 \text{ lbs. } 8 \text{ ozs.} \\ \hline \end{array}$$

what kinds of problems are missed, but it does not tell *why they were missed*. It therefore leaves out a very necessary type of information. The proper companion of paper and pencil diagnosis is the individual interview. The interview supplies the missing data.

In the individual interview the teacher systematically sits down with one child at a time and has him think out loud in working the problem, so that the source of the difficulty can be discovered. One child had consistently missed problems in column addition for two years, without anyone discovering the reason for her difficulty.

Finally the difficulty was quickly pointed up by a teacher who had the child think out loud for her. What the student had done for two years, or longer, was to add the first column for her partial sum which she added correctly. Then, however, she always carried one to the next column regardless of the size of the partial sum. No one knew how she came to develop this error, but the interview technique revealed what was wrong and the difficulty was corrected.

Observation of the teaching of arithmetic seems to indicate that diagnosis does not play the important role it deserves. A qualitative program involves considerably more than diagnosis, and in those schools where test-teach-test is the mathematical diet, diagnosis is overdone and the program is impoverished. No program of mathematics, however, can achieve maximum efficiency without the judicious use of diagnosis.

Problem-Solving

If an 8 oz. can of sauerkraut costs 16¢ and a 16 oz. can costs 29¢ which is the better buy? Nine out of ten students will be inclined to say that the 16 oz. can is the better buy, and divorced from reality, that is the logical answer. Placed within the framework of real circumstances, however, it may not be the answer at all. For the fact of the matter is that it depends on whether or not one likes sauerkraut.

Problem-solving in modern times has shown refreshing improvement in the degree to which the content has been made more realistic. The older textbooks in arithmetic were full of highly improbable problem situations which were of somewhat the same cloth and vintage as the discussion of how many angels could rest on the point of a needle. Problem-solving in modern schools stays closer to life as children know it, and is not only more practical but more significant as well.

The basic purpose of arithmetic in the curriculum is ordinarily identified as the development of children's abilities to think quantitatively. This has reference to all thinking which involves numbers and number relationships. Problem-solving, thus, is right at the heart of the curricular role. It is a reflection of the child's ability to come to grips with real problems of living, utilizing what he has learned in one situation and applying it to another. It involves careful assessment of the facts and circumstances, and logical and sometimes even creative application of reasoning to the desired end. This is a highly prized aspect of the development of modern man, and deserves the school's best effort to achieve it. What elements in the program will highlight and nourish this vital factor?

In terms of what has been recommended as qualitative elements thus far, the stage is already set for such achievement. Promoting the self-discovery approach, building up the conceptual materials, stressing functional applications to the day-by-day operation, and highlighting the pervading function of diagnosis are all compatible and contributing to problem-solving. Each of these factors embraces the same spirit and intent, but in themselves may not be enough.

Typically, children of the elementary school do better in computation than in problem-solving because the typical classroom stresses it more. One can teach what one chooses to emphasize. One aspect of improved problem-solving is simply to place more stress on it. If the total budget of time slights problem-solving in favor of mere computational arithmetic, this situation should be reversed.

Another factor which has traditionally stood in the way of better problem-solving is the ability of the child to read. The ability to read critically and with understanding is interlocked with problem-solving at this point. The reading lessons might properly draw from the arithmetic texts for specific focus on the thought-type problems, in order to improve understanding and skills of this nature.

A third way to achieve a degree of improvement is to concentrate more carefully on fewer, more selectively chosen problems. In a way this is like the assignment of themes. Other things being equal, it would be better to have a total of six themes in a semester that were carefully written, polished, and qualitatively improved, than to write two or three times that number that were dealt with in cursory fashion. All adults can recall being assigned one or more pages of written problems that were chorelike in nature and not really very important to them. Five carefully selected problems might easily provide for the desired types to be focused upon in a given period, and also allow for ample time to dwell upon the intrinsic nature of each. There should be time for children to interpret different ways of arriving at their solutions, and the thoughtful comparison and weighing of their approaches. Much of the arithmetic instruction throughout the nation is too hurried. Mathematics is a thoughtful process and must be so conducted without someone breathing down the child's neck with a stopwatch. Five problems, as an example, could even provide challenge for the more gifted by choosing them in terms of increasing difficulty. The fifth one might be a one-hundred megaton type. The point being that the number assigned should be chosen with the idea of doing each of them thoroughly and right. The number would obviously vary with the nature of the content and should be flexible. In some instances even one problem might suffice.

Whatever form the brave new world of mathematics takes in the elementary school in years to come, problem-solving will still be of major importance. It now is, and will continue to be, one of the major qualitative factors.

Acceleration

A traditional teacher in a traditional school became dissatisfied with her classes in arithmetic. She taught in a departmentalized form of organization and was responsible for the teaching of arithmetic in grades four, five, and six. Her children were somewhat below average in intelligence, were disinterested in arithmetic, and in her opinion were making little or no progress. On the assumption that she had nothing to lose, she reorganized her program. She went through her texts pulling out what she thought were the most central or essential learnings, and summarized these into a very selective and carefully planned list of assignments. The assignments were recorded on three by five cards and placed in a file box in the corner of the room.

She then went before her classes and told them quite candidly that their progress in arithmetic to date had been unsatisfactory, and that they would from this point on be using a different approach. She interpreted the assignment cards for them, told them that each pupil could work at the assignments at his own rate, and told them to go to work.

The children very quickly began to spread out in their progress; some at the end of the second week had completed the tenth assignment, while others were still on assignment two. The teacher used her time in three important ways. She would move around the room helping individual children as they needed help; she would call aside a small group of children who might be ready to move into a new topic and carefully introduce the topic to them; and she would call aside those who had completed a given group of assignments in order to check them on what they had learned. If they could not show understanding and mastery they were not permitted to go on to the next step.

The most tangible evidence of some degree of success with her plan was the change in attitude of the students. They came alive. In fact, other teachers complained that the children were overmotivated, for they would take their arithmetic books to their other classes to do the next card. Teachers of language arts and social studies were less than delighted about this. Nevertheless, the project continued, and by the end of six months the classes had each chalked up impressive gains as measured by the standardized tests used by the school.

What is the point to an approach of this kind? Perhaps the most obvious advantage is the pacing; the children quickly spread out. They are allowed to set their own levels of aspiration and to work accordingly. This is precisely what the newly emerging teaching machines will accomplish and they will serve a vital purpose. This teacher used a somewhat crude version of a teaching machine and made it work, even thought she was handicapped in providing the degree of instant reinforcement of learning that characterizes the modern technology.

One of the dominant trends in the programs of arithmetic in the next few years will be acceleration of the program. This acceleration is inevitable. One aspect of acceleration is to bring down into the lower grades form and content in mathematics that was formerly thought to be appropriate for only older students. Some schools have already experimented with the teaching of geometry to seven year olds. The emergence of set theory in the primary grades will orient children to arithmetic in such a manner that youngsters will have the prelude to higher forms of mathematics. It is probably too early to predict the effect of this change. Early reports are enthusiastic, but they need to be weighed in a larger context. The degree to which one can teach set theory in the first three years of schooling may be so inconsequential as to make it for all practical purposes a waste of time—and when one is teaching this, he is not teaching something else. Better research may yet indicate that in his first three years of school the child would be more enriched by learning a second language, and spending his time for mathematics primarily in a higher and more intelligent level of functional mathematics as a solid underpinning for heavier mathematics beginning in grade four. The answer to this is not yet known, even though some mathematicians may give the impression that it is a settled matter. The schools today must be careful not to allow this trend to degenerate into the exploitation of the elementary school for the sole benefit of higher mathematics at some later date.

Be that as it may, the second aspect of acceleration has to do with more mathematics for all the children. The hazard here is that many of the children already have all they are able to handle. The safeguard of the wisely used teaching machine is that the pacing can be individualized. Those who can do more do, and those who can't are not required to. This is the kind of acceleration which seems most compatible with the image of the qualitative elementary school.

Mathematics for Fun

A seventh grade teacher in the Phoenix Elementary Schools has a worthwhile practice which he uses two or three times a week with his class just before he dismisses them for the day. He gave them problems that were "just for fun." The following is an example of one of the problems he gave his class:

A primary teacher had in her first grade a very bright boy who was always finishing his work before the other children and coming up to ask what he could do next. It was difficult for the teacher to keep him busy, but she was usually able to provide something constructive for him to do. One day, however, she was particularly pressed and harrassed and was caught unprepared. Therefore, she gave the child a piece of busy work which she tried ordinarily to avoid. She asked the boy to go back to his seat and write the numbers from one to one-hundred, then to add them and bring her the correct sum. The child went to his seat and was busy for about sixty seconds. Then he came happily back and handed her the correct answer. How did the child work the problem?

The students in this particular class have a high degree of interest in mathematics and they particularly look forward to these occasional problems. It adds a touch of zest to their mathematical diet and provides an additional stimulus to thought. It even constitutes an example of a type of homework which is completely palatable to students. The teacher of this class is a scholarly, well-rounded young man who can have a wholesome and lasting influence on his students' lives. He has selectively through the years developed a very interesting collection of stimulating problems and keeps adding to them as he goes along. He is not a mathematician, but he is developing mathematical interests in his students.

Mathematics is an area of the curriculum which is to be "beefed up" in the years to come, and there is a danger that it may become a stolid and musclebound segment of the program. The nature of the beefing up process will make the difference. The fun factor is a safeguard against such a potential danger. It is also an incentive to creativity, for many of the fun-type problems such as the one above offer several possible answers.

There is an additional reason, however, for suggesting that this element be deliberately built into the program. In what other way can mathematics become a part of people's lives to the degree that a modern technical society demands? It is not enough for a society to have an elite corps of well trained mathematicians who carry on its highly specialized processes, and at the same time allow the rest of society to be mathematical paupers. The nation requires a better mathematical posture than this, and the factor under discussion is one of the avenues for developing it. Such a factor has a unique contribution to make to the quality of the program.

Summary

Mathematics in the elementary school seems to be on the verge of some revolutionary changes. The nature of this change is not yet in clear enough focus to project it in this interpretation. The broad ideas chosen for emphasis here, therefore, are those which seem to reflect some of the best of the current practices. These ideas are sufficiently important to warrant the opinion that they will probably continue to be a prominent part of the mathematics to come. Thus, the selective factors may constitute a sort of link between the old and the new. Seven broad ideas have been developed, and the qualitative program is interpreted as one which:

1. Continues to stress meaning and self-discovery in its approach.
2. Develops and uses conceptual aids as an intrinsic part of the meaning approach.
3. Provides for systematic use of functional arithmetic.
4. Makes *judicious* use of diagnosis.
5. Emphasizes problem-solving over mere computation.
6. Provides an accelerated program for those who should accelerate.
7. Tempers the "beefing up" process by filtering fun throughout the total program.

Chapter 8

Creativity

If the attributes that are most vital to a free society were to be placed in a hierarchy of importance, creativity would rank very high. Creativity constitutes the growth edge of a system of free enterprise, and adds immeasurably to the enrichment of personal living. The creativity of two or three individuals may well have tipped the scales in favor of the Allies in World War II, and the outcome of the cold war could be decided on the same basis. Creativity is linked, therefore, not only to a refinement of the quality of living, but to a preservation of the way of life itself.

The anomaly of the situation is that vital as creativity seems to be to the national destiny there is no concerted effort to sustain or nourish it. The creative child is not likely to be appreciated by his teacher and may even incur her active dislike. The creative adult finds two basically unattractive alternatives awaiting him. On the one hand, he will probably not be promoted as rapidly as his more conforming associates. On the other hand, if he is promoted he will then be expected to assume additional routine responsibilities which diminish his creative output. In general, the society as well as the schools have failed to attach sufficient importance to identifying their more creative members, and to structuring a setting in which creativity may most advantageously flourish. A continuation of this condition could assume the proportions of a national tragedy.

One of the interesting discoveries of modern psychology is that creativity does not appear to be positively correlated with intelligence. If one attempts to select the most creative members of a group by choosing those who score highest on common measures of intelligence, he will fail to include more than two-thirds of the most creative members. The perceptive layman has suspected this for a long time, but the psychologist has only recently caught up with him and verified it. The real truth of the matter may lie not in the lack of correlation between creativity and intelligence but in the deficiencies of the evaluating instruments themselves. For the present measures of intelligence may simply be incapable of appraising *the most vital aspects* of what they are attempting to assess.

It is not the intent of this discussion to interpret creativity in any unusual or special sense. The essence of creativity seems to involve uniqueness of response. At a fairly common level of uniqueness of response one is dealing simply with individuality, for individuality is that aspect of behavior which is a unique expression of the self. At a higher level of expression uniqueness of response may emerge in the form of new devices, inventions, solutions, or thoughts. Individuality is a sort of growing ground for higher levels of creative expression. The more individuality exists in a given situation the more likelihood there is that new forms and ideas will develop. Individuality may then be said to feed the creative process.

The elementary school has a very vital role to play in any kind of concerted effort to foster creativity. For although the twig is already bent before the child comes to school, he is still in a formative stage, and it is the earliest opportunity available to the school to nurture whatever creative impulses he may possess. In fact, any point beyond the elementary years may even prove to be too late. His approach to life and his manner of thinking are rapidly being shaped, and they should be shaped in the image of a creative individual. Five factors which are believed to be important in the development of a creative personality are interpreted in the following. Each factor has reference and application to each child in the classroom rather than to a favored few. This is due in part to the fact that there is no way at the present time to accurately select the most favored few. More substantially, it is due to the recognition that each child has some capacity for creativity, and that it is the proper business of the elementary school to develop it.

Environmental Richness

Thirty children in a fifth grade class were given a simple mathematical problem involving scores on spelling. The five scores given were 85, 90, 95, 80, and 100. Twenty-nine of the children added the scores and divided the sum by five. The remaining child simply looked at the scores and jotted down the answer. He had mentally added 15, 10, 5, and 20, divided that sum by five, and subtracted from 100 to arrive at the average. His teacher frowned at him and seemed displeased with what he had done. It was reminiscent of the fable of the Animal School. In that delightful fable the eagle surpassed all of the competing animals in getting to the top of the tree, but was criticized for using his own method of getting there.

Environmental richness is a sort of total thrust. Creativity is not *imprisoned in the art period,* as it may be in so many schools. It is nourished throughout the curriculum wherever the opportunities for being creative may occur. In the above incident the child had never been taught to compute an average in that manner. His prior mathematical instruction, however, had emphasized meaning and self-discovery, so his inclination toward a unique method of solving the problem was greater than it might otherwise have been. Many learning activities throughout the program may contribute to this total thrust. Thus, meaning and self-discovery as a qualitative ingredient in elementary mathematics makes a contribution to creativity. The attempt to resolve their own problems of everyday living in social studies affords children opportunity and practice in bringing creativity to bear on their own affairs. The nurture of scientific thinking in science, and even the thought approach to spelling strengthen the capacity for creative response. When the many opportunities for individuality of thinking and approach are utilized throughout the program one is extending the total thrust. Without this general push a school cannot adequately develop creativity any more than it can develop adequate language usage in a "language period."

Another aspect of environmental richness is reflected by materials and media for expression. A school that limits children's creative experiences to paper and crayons is as impoverished and barren as the classroom in which the question-answer recitation is the sole method of instruction. One of the encouraging aspects of the modern school is the manner in which it has selectively extended the child's experiences with a variety of media. Children in the better schools have opportunities to work with wood, leather, clay, finger paint, puppetry, poetry, dancing, and a host of other materials and media. One or more of these will surely light a spark for everyone, so that each child in the classroom is more likely to find a satisfying means of bringing out his thoughts and feelings about his world.

Environmental richness is thus a general enrichment of the soil. Its purpose is to provide one of the basic conditions for stimulating creative response in each child. Even more significantly, it enlarges the arena in which creativity may occur and apply. It is a distinctive and essential characteristic of quality in the excellent school.

Sensory Awareness

Creativity seems to be linked to sensory awareness. Beethoven could walk by the sea or through the forest and experience such a perceptual awareness of sound and mood that he could recreate it in his music. Civilized man may have less sensory awareness than his primitive forbears for it is less essential to his survival. Then, too, many of the man-made aspects of his environment must be deliberately tuned out in order to maintain his sanity. He learns to selectively tune out certain noises, odors, and irritations as an essential aspect of adjusting to the circumstances of his existence. Thus, sensory awareness is dulled and becomes one of the casualties of modern civilization. It seems imperative at the same time, however, that one not dull his basic capacity for response.

Sensory awareness needs to be sharpened or heightened in the elementary school in order to maintain and develop the child's capacity for adequate response to his environment. This is a part of being fully alive, and of being a fully developed individual. There are adults who can walk in the woods without hearing the birds sing, who can look at a setting sun as they drive home from work without seeing the sunset, or who can walk down the street after a spring rain without feeling the freshness of the earth. This blunting of the senses is neither necessary nor desirable, and represents a shriveling of the organism. Such an individual is only partially alive. The qualitative teacher will not allow this partial death to take place in his room. He will keep a portion of the child's experiences in intimate contact with the natural wonders of the world, and he will actively seek to extend and heighten the senses themselves.

There are no well-marked trails for the heightening of the senses. It is an aspect of teaching in which one's own imagination and sensitivities may be the best guide. To emphasize the sense of feel one teacher brought to her class an object buried under pieces of cut paper in the bottom of a sack. Each child was allowed to feel the mystery object briefly and to guess what it might be. No doubt the last child to feel it had a quite different sensation than the first, for the thoughtful examination by twenty-nine pairs of hands had radically altered its external characteristics. The object was an orange. A science teacher worked at the heightening of the senses by shutting off one of them temporarily. As an introduction to a unit on sight he arranged for his students to do without sight for twenty-four hours by having their eyes taped. Students who experienced this procedure felt that they could see more after the removal of the blind, in addition to having a keener appreciation for the sense of sight itself. A primary teacher worked at increasing her children's perceptions by blindfolding one child at a time and having him guess which of his classmates was speaking to him. Wide trait differences were apparent in this procedure, but more significantly, the accuracy of perception seemed to increase with practice.

In a qualitative school the activities designed to heighten perceptual awareness would be a conscious and discernible part of the curriculum. At the present time such activity in the schools seems almost nonexistent. This is probably because verbal activities tend to dominate such a considerable portion of the curriculum. In a verbal society verbal activities are a significant part of an individual's development—but alone, they can lead only to a maladjusted and malfunctioning man. The vigorous, alert, fully alive person has all of his antennae working. His sensory equipment is in full contact with his environment, and this in turn accents the degree to which he can achieve intellectual development. Creativity is enhanced by this process.

Imagination

Imagination is the magic carpet of childhood, and one of the great compensating mechanisms of life is that it is distributed rather equally between the rich and the poor. A child who has not saved the elephant herds with Tarzan, or tramped the Himalayas with Hillary, or made his own contacts with the visitors from outer space is surely living too sedately for his own welfare. But imagination is not merely a child's pass to the magnificent dimension of make-believe. For the adult it is a continuing link between the present and the future. It is a bridge between the world of today and what it may eventually come to be. Many of the breathtaking advancements of today were spawned first in the imagination of creative men. First the dream, then the reality—this is the sequence exemplified by some of the most creative men and women of our generation. Henry Kaiser is a remarkable practitioner of this sequence. He may awaken at four A.M. with such a compelling idea that he leaps out of bed to start phoning his friends. His approach to life is summarized in the expression "living a dream fulfilled."

One of the most creative teachers of our times was once asked to define imagination. He thought for a moment and then said simply that it was *the ability to think of things as they are not.* There is a considerable tendency in the elementary schools to think of things as they are, but almost no effort to think of them as they are not. This is an imbalance which frequently escapes attention in the schools as they attempt to shore up their defenses and teach more science and mathematics. Yet, imagination is vital in both science and mathematics. It is doubtful that Einstein could have even conceived his unified field theory without an active assist from his imagination, and Applegate has aptly described a scientist as one "who builds a ladder in the air and then climbs it even though it isn't there."

A fourth grade teacher in the Southwest plays a little game orally with her children. She will ask them to imagine that they are unusual objects and to speak as this object might speak if it had the power to communicate. For instance, she will ask them to reflect the feelings of the unwritten side of a sheet of paper, a squeaky board on a stairway, a sunken ship off Santa Barbara, the last chocolate in a box, or the clown's hat after the party.

It is difficult to see how time spent on some of the fairy stories read in the elementary schools makes any significant contribution to the development of children's imagination. What contribution for instance is made by the story of Hansel and Gretel? It is a macabre affair from the initial cruelty of the stepmother right on through to the cremation of the witch. Wouldn't the time spent on unfortunate material of this nature be better devoted to oral and written stories that are the active projections of the child's own imagination? With some children it may be necessary to tell a portion of a most interesting story and allow them to determine the ending. With other children a single provocative idea may be all that is required to set thoughts racing over an uncharted course.

A teacher's effort to stimulate the imagination of her children is often considered a sort of educational fluff. This is particularly true in the vast community of the uninformed. The qualitative school, however, whether it exists among the informed or the uninformed, will manage to keep imagination alive. For imagination is the Great Eye that sees beyond what is known, the Giant Searchlight that brings the unknown into focus, and the forerunner of research and hypothesis. It is, also, the indispensable ingredient of creativity.

Beauty

Until recently, one could climb a small hill in Papago Park near Phoenix and look down on a vast expanse of desert beauty. To the East lay the majestic Superstition Mountains shrouded in mystery and grandeur. And between Papago and the Superstitions was mile after mile of natural desert dotted with the giant saguaro that stand like lonely sentinels on an eternal vigil. For those who were responsive to the simple charm of the desert it was an area of enchantment and loveliness.

The view is different now. As one approaches the rise of the hill his senses are shocked by row after row of identical reflecting rooftops standing in stark and ugly contrast to the scene below. This did not need to be. Imagination and a sensitivity to beauty could easily have varied the structures and blended them into the landscape. Perhaps the developer attended "art classes" in an elementary school where all of the children made identical looking tulips. If so, society has now reaped its commensurate reward, and another area of natural beauty is forever lost to what is inaccurately labeled as progress.

In the main, the marks that man has made upon his environment do not reflect a sensitivity to beauty. He has destroyed much that is lovely and replaced it with very little in return. He has carved fine highways into areas of natural splendor and then punctuated the view with offensive advertising. He has developed retreats in the wilderness for those who wish to escape civilization, and then littered them with beer cans and other sordid reminders of the civilization he sought to escape. He has blackened the cities, fouled the streams, and is now diligently engaged in corrupting the entire atmosphere. In his personal affairs his score is not much better. He will wear brown shoes with a blue suit, and join a bowling club instead of the art league. Even his home, which is supposed to be his castle, tends to be built in the general architectural style of an outhouse. The silhouette is lower and the square footage is increased, but otherwise the structures are much the same. In tribute to man, however, he has insisted in recent times on adding a picture window even though it must look out upon the local pool hall.

The above contains some exaggeration, of course, and man is not really this insensitive to beauty. He builds an oasis here and there, and occasionally one runs across a home, or a neighborhood, or a public building which really enhances the area in which it stands. But these are not commonplace; in fact they are so uncommon as to attract attention and comment. Obviously, therefore, the sensitivity to beauty that is reflected by the common man leaves much to be desired. It is a situation that seems to cry out for improvement.

Beauty is not synonymous with creativity, of course, for creativity can produce the nonbeautiful as well as the beautiful. But the intent of this discussion is to suggest that creativity *should consciously embrace beauty and project it in the man-made environment.* If, among other benefits, the world is not to be lovelier as a result of increased creativity, then something in the process has misfired. Children should learn in the elementary school to bring more beauty into their surroundings and into their lives.

As a case in point, the typical primary teacher makes an effort to have her room attractively arranged before the children arrive. One kindergarten teacher, however, rejected this idea. Her room was barren when the children arrived because she believed that the children themselves should undertake the job of making their room more beautiful. Their room, when it was finished, did not have a ready-made look, and it was not arranged in terms of the standards of an adult. But the room was warm and pleasing to them, and they grew in their understanding and sensitivity to beauty. Over the long haul such an approach should come much closer to producing a generation of adults that possesses the sensitivities this one seems to lack. Beauty should be fused through the life of children. They should have experiences in replacing drabness with something better. Each child should develop a feeling of responsibility for adding in some way to the total store of beauty that exists in the world. Beauty should be learned as a pervading concept that embraces thoughts and gracious acts as well as more material things. And beauty should be consciously sought, consciously created, and consciously shared. This is a significant contribution to life which is made by the qualitative school.

Creative Teaching

One of the schools in a large district in the Midwest was located in what is often described as the wrong side of the tracks. The children in this school enjoyed the blessing of some creative teachers, however, and had the reputation of producing creative work. One year the school served as host for a state conference, and in preparation for the event the children's art was attractively displayed throughout the building. Teachers from all over the state came to this conference and admired the fresh and original work of the children. Several of them then went to the principal and asked "Where can we get the patterns for this art work?"

Fortunately, all elementary children are not in the custody of teachers who are this deficient in their concept of creativity. The first grade children in a laboratory school came to their room one morning in September and found some strange "tracks" on their papers. There was much speculation about what might have caused them but no facts. The next morning they were there again, and because they were very small and shaped like a human foot, the children concluded that their room may have been visited by a Brownie. On the basis of this tentative conclusion they drafted a note to their nocturnal visitor asking him if he would like to live in their room. His reply was in such small print that it had to be read under a magnifying glass. He inquired cautiously about the rent. The children decided that a Brownie might not have much money so they set the rent at two cents. He decided that at that figure he could stay, and a lively correspondence was established in the first few weeks of school. In the late fall their Brownie visited Oak

Creek one weekend, and brought the children beautifully colored leaves. As Christmas drew near he had to leave for a period of time to help Santa, and he rode gloriously to the North Pole on the wings of a redbird.

Although the children could only see their Brownie in the "mind's eye" he was a discernible part of their curriculum. He helped bridge the gap between home and school during the first days. He caused them to want to write, and to read what they had written. He added some color and incentive to their day. In conception and application this teaching was creative.

Creative teaching seems to defy formulas and is rarely fostered by the implementation of specific techniques. One of the basic purposes of unit teaching was to free the teacher from the regimentation of a text, and to inspire a freer and more creative approach. Yet, any close observer of the scene recognizes that unit teaching often became as compulsive and rigid as the form it sought to replace. Creative teaching is the function of creative individuals, and the teaching can only be as creative as the individual who conceives it. The creative teacher has an awareness of the common techniques of his profession, but is less dependent on them. He dos not ignore the well-marked trails of other teachers, but strives to improve them. He understands the fundamental processes of given ap-approaches to teaching, but frequently transcends them.

If a school wishes to make the assumption that creative development of children is positively affected by creative teaching, there are two basic roads to improvement. One road is to selectively recruit the most creative teachers that can be obtained. These teachers will not be revealed by grade point averages or intelligence quotients. They are more likely to be revealed by classroom performance, interview, and candid appraisal of themselves in regard to their creative drives. The other road to improvement involves the creating of conditions that enable all teachers to be as creative as they would like to be. This involves removal of the penalties and fears of making a mistake, official encouragement to strike out with new ways, and active administrative assistance in the expediting of materials and ideas. It is reasonable to assume that there is a great reservoir of creative capacities in teachers that is largely unused. The administrator of a qualitative school will tap these unused resources and bring them into fuller play, for this is one of the significant ways in which he can contribute to increased creativity in his generation.

Summary

Creativity has been interpreted as uniqueness of response, which at higher levels of expressions is reflected in the form of new ideas, inventions, or other original projections of the human mind. Creativity is a vital aspect of the development of an individual in terms of the enrichment and fulfillment of the total self. It is equally vital, however, to the perpetuation and survival of the society itself. Although creativity is of such importance as to justify its emphasis at all levels of the curriculum, it is of special importance to stress it in the elementary school. This is because the twig is still green at this stage, and can be directed in the image of a more creative individual. The philosophy of the approach in the elementary school is that an emphasis on creativity should be beamed at all of the children, on the assumption that all of them have some degree of creativity to be developed. This approach is realistic in the additional sense that those children with the most capacity for creativity cannot be accurately identified with present instruments of selection or evaluation. Five factors which are believed to be particularly significant for emphasis in the elementary school have been interpreted. Thus, the qualitative school will foster creativity when it:

1. Utilizes the total creative thrust of the curriculum.
2. Works actively to heighten the senses themselves.
3. Provides special opportunities for children to think of things "as they are not."
4. Cultivates a sensitivity and responsibility for beauty in living.
5. Encourages and increases the incidence of creative teaching.

Chapter 9

Discipline

If a parent or a teacher seems confused about discipline today he is showing encouraging signs of normalcy, for one would have to be moronic or alarmingly insensitive to complacently assimilate the conflicting claims and testimony on this important topic. On the one hand, he hears the harsh and strident voices urging him to get tough with the young punks, to shave their heads, administer public floggings, and subject them to humiliation and ridicule. On the other hand, he hears the gentle voices pleading for more love and understanding, telling him that there is no such thing as a problem child—there are only children with problems. The hapless individual may meditate on the matter, and being basically a humanitarian he develops in his heart a great kindness and feeling of compassion for these youngsters with problems. Then one night they waylay him in the park, or burn down his house, or club his invalid grandmother; and the next day he is urging shaved heads, public floggings, and other forms of humiliation and ridicule.

Rousseau's dream of the "noble savage" has appealed to many who favor the relaxation of discipline and authority in society. As one looks realistically at juvenile gangsters and hoodlums, however, it is obvious that they are more savage than noble. They have fed on the weaknesses of society and have become a threat, if not a malignancy. At this advanced stage of the cancer it is too late for the gentle voices to be effective. The application of softness to hardened young criminals is as inadequate as the hypothesis of the Philosophical Cat. This cat roamed the jungle eating birds in order

115

to become more birdlike. Naturally, he did not become more bird-like; he merely became a larger cat.

The Swiss, who almost alone among the nations do not have a burgeoning rate of delinquency on their hands, are amazed at the corrupting influences to which this nation allows its young people to be subjected. They do not permit the minds of their children to be penetrated by the sex and violence of movies and television and they cannot understand why America continues to do so. Delinquency is a complex matter which will not be solved by turning off the television. It has an intricate root system, and probably mirrors the innermost condition of the society itself. Delinquency can be reduced, however, by a more adequate and enlightened approach in the early years.

In the discussion which follows, discipline is regarded as the quality of the human relationships which prevail. Discipline obviously has many legitimate concerns, some of which are considerably more important than others. In the old days of teacher education the neophyte teacher was cautioned to stand in such a position that she could see every child in the room, and to "ride her eye over the class." The writer's view of this admonition is that if the relationship of a teacher and her class is as bankrupt as this, it would be better for everyone to go home. The factors selected for interpretation here hope to be more significant ones. Thus, the discussion includes Watson's revealing report on permissiveness, Jersild's sensitive view of self-control, a forthright concept of authority by Margaret Mead, and the haunting remarks of Lao Tze on rules.

From such commonplace matters a very special effort has been made to pull out aspects that are of unusual or enduring consequence. Most parents and teachers already know a great deal about discipline, but they need to take their bearings frequently and to reaffirm their views. To that end, the six ideas which follow should be helpful. They bring to the deliberation of everyday matters some special considerations which should be of interest to all concerned.

Permissiveness

One of the most provocative pieces of research of modern times was the four year study of permissiveness carried out by the Columbia University Council for Research in the Social Sciences. This important study attempted to answer the question of whether it is better to grow up in a permissive or a strict home.[1]

A strict home had reference to the kind in which parents would feed babies on a regular schedule, insist on clean hands and good table manners, toilet train babies early, make children keep their possessions orderly, etc. The strict parent was interpreted as one who believed·

You should make your children form good habits and teach them definitely what is expected of them; good behavior should be approved and bad behavior punished.

A permissive home had reference to the kind in which parents would follow self-demand schedules with babies, and later let children eat largely whenever and whatever they pleased. Toilet training was delayed until the child himself wanted it, and children were allowed to keep their toys as messy or as orderly as they wished. The permissive parent was interpreted as one who believed:

Children can well make most of their decisions for themselves, and parents should respect the child's developing inner self-direction. Children need freedom and their experience will tell them what works out well and what does not. They will naturally model themselves after their parents if they love them. Scolding and spanking do more harm than good.

In other words, the homes involved in the study were selected with the specific idea in mind of being in marked contrast to one another so far as permissiveness itself was concerned. Otherwise, the homes, whether strict or permissive, were good homes where children were wanted and received plenty of love. Care was taken not to confuse permissiveness with carelessness, or strictness with harshness or cruelty. The study reports that it proved much easier to find very strict homes than very permissive ones. Finally, 38 permissive homes were found to be acceptable and a matching number of strict homes were used.

The children were then turned over to psychologists for observation and study. The psychologists, of course, did not know which children were from which type of home. The following results were reported:

1. Children from the permissive homes were more creative than children from strict homes by a ratio of 7 to 1.

[1] Goodwin Watson, "The Spoiled Child," *McCalls*, May, 1958.

2. Children from permissive homes were found to be more independent and self-reliant by a ratio of 6 to 1.
3. The most socialized, cooperative, and best accepted youngsters came from permissive homes by a ratio of 3 to 1.
4. With respect to problem-solving, children from strict homes tended to quit prematurely on a difficult task, or else to keep trying the same thing over and over again beyond the point of intelligence. By contrast, the children from permissive homes worked at a difficult task a reasonable length of time and then gave up. They were less likely to give up quickly, and less likely to keep trying beyond the point of intelligence. They would try varied approaches until they had exhausted their repertoire, and then give up instead of repeating moves which would not work.

How should one regard this research? It presents permissiveness in a most favorable light; for if one were to deliberately set out to identify qualities more vital to our way of life than creativity, self-reliance, cooperation, and problem-solving, it would be difficult to come up with a more impressive list. Yet, permissiveness is widely maligned in almost every circle and every walk of life. Along with "togetherness" and "life-adjustment," it is ridiculed and pilloried as one of the arch villains of our times.

Is permissiveness part of the rich, black soil that children need in order to grow? Is it, like sunshine, a basic ingredient that is necessary for one to become his best self? Many schools have already thrown permissiveness out of their curriculum, and others are preparing to do so. Perhaps they should take a second and more thoughtful look at the matter. The present reaction to misguided permissiveness has created a mood in which there is danger of throwing out the baby with the bath. What is popular cannot be equated with what is right. The writer believes that in a qualitative approach to discipline the sunlight of an enlightened permissiveness will continue to play a vital role in the program.

Play Therapy

Patricia was a child in the first grade of a small elementary school. She was slightly overage for her grade, and was larger and stronger than her classmates. Her behavior was often strange and unpredictable. For instance, she might suddenly for no apparent reason leap out of her seat and strike a child in the next aisle. This particular room had three swings available to the children at recess, and no matter where Patricia might be in the line that formed to go out for play she would manage to get one of the swings—she might leave, however, a trail of piled-up bodies in her wake. She was unclean, and even unwholesome looking. She was not learning to read or allowing anyone else much opportunity to do so, and her teacher went to the principal and threw in the towel. Here, in the words of the principal, is what happened:

> Patricia was of such an unwholesome appearance that I must confess I did not want to work with her. I took the case simply because it was my job to do so. Although no one should feel this way about a child, Patricia was repulsive to me.
>
> Actually I had no more idea as to what to do with her than her teacher. I had just read Virginia Axline's splendid little book on *Play Therapy*,[2] however, and since it seemed that there was very little to lose, decided to give it a try.
>
> There was no play therapy equipment in the school so it was necessary to use the supplies that were on hand. Patricia came to me three afternoons a week for one half hour at a time. She worked with finger paint, drew pictures, made up stories which she told to me, and in general just let go. The half hour was exclusively hers. I did not answer the phone or permit any interruptions to the session. I tried to make her comfortable, tried to follow her leads, tried to be responsive to the emotional rather than the intellectual content of her remarks, and scrupulously avoided any of the adult prerogatives that characterize the relationship of a principal to a child.
>
> Gradually Patricia opened up. Gradually she began to shed the outer layers of personality and bared her inner self. As this took place I suddenly realized that I no longer saw her as a repulsive child. Can the feeling that someone is repulsive actually make them more so? Can losing the thought actually help the condition to disappear? Patricia seemed to undergo a marked change. She responded differently to her classmates and teacher, and they responded differently to her. Everyone who knew about Patricia was amazed. It seemed that a minor miracle had taken place.

No one will ever know what caused the minor miracle of change described by Patricia's principal. Perhaps she just started to grow up. Perhaps the transformation that took place would have occurred without the crude therapy that was contrived for her. But no one intimately associated with the child believed that to be true. All

---

[2] Virginia Axline, *Play Therapy*, Boston, Houghton Mifflin, 1947.

who knew of the case attributed the change to the special procedures that were used.

Play therapy is an arrangement which places a child in a specially planned setting where he can be more free. In this special environment of freedom he can be obscene, he can have tantrums and hurl himself on the floor, he can pull the head off a doll which resembles his baby sister, or take a dummy of his stepfather and beat it to a bloody pulp. In short, he can externalize the feelings which have piled up inside of him. There are definite things that he cannot do. He cannot strike the therapist, or abuse another child, or break windows. But the boundaries of permissiveness are greatly extended in this special setting, and he is given as much latitude as it is possible to provide.

Play therapy is a *controlled form of permissiveness*, for the deliberate extension of what the child may do takes place only in a specific location and at a prearranged time. One of the fascinating lessons learned from early experiences with play therapy was that a child who can get things off his chest in the regular session of play therapy does not need to do those things when he goes back into his classroom. If one accepts the fact that permissiveness per se is an important ingredient of the qualitative school, but that it needs to be delimited and controlled, then play therapy is one of the answers.

There is another significant outlet, however, quite aside from play therapy as such. If one really understands the spirit and intent of permissiveness, he can provide for it within the regular classroom sessions without ordinarily resorting to special facilities. The normal curriculum abounds in opportunities for guided permissiveness in creative writing, creative play, in puppetry, dramatics, in music and art and dance. The opportunities are there, to be extracted and distilled by the discerning and thoughtful teacher who knows what he is about. The proper exploitation of these opportunities is a subtle but powerful factor in the discipline of the qualitative school.

Self-Control

In Jersild's study of the search for self, he found that many young people listed a lack of self-control as one of the characteristics which they disliked about themselves. He believed that they were showing the influence of a training designed to persuade them not to be emotional, and that they were playing up to the ideal of being a strong, silent, dispassionate, and Spartan-like personality.[3]

In its best meaning, self-control is healthy and constructive—best, if it means the ability to respond in a way that is appropriate, and that one has at his command a good store of feeling for self and others. What is not generally recognized, however, is that *the more a person possesses such capacities for response the less need he has to control himself.*

Jersild believes that the idea of control in the form it often takes is false and morbid. One will keep a stiff upper lip; he will not give way, he will suffer in silence, he will not lose his temper. If he possesses this false notion of control he will not allow himself to weep in sorrow, or cry out in rage, or tremble with fear, or shout with joy. If he is on the brink of an experience so charged with emotion that he could both laugh and cry, he will catch himself and do neither. For he must at all cost put up a good front, always reply "fine" when someone asks how he is, and always keep smiling.

To Jersild, such a concept of emotional maturity is threadbare and pernicious. Maturity and control are not the same. What passes for control of emotion is instead the absence of emotion. Such a person has never grown up or matured in his ability to relate himself wholeheartedly to others. One who has curtailed his development in this manner has surrendered to a stereotype, and is taking place in a masquerade. He leads a life so barren that he cannot weep with compassion, for he feels none. He cannot rise in righteous anger in the face of abuse, for he has surrendered his right to be angry.

Many teachers and parents seem to perpetuate the false and unhealthy concept of control that is so aptly described by Jersild. The qualitative elementary school will not subject children to such an emotionally deprived setting. Instead, it will nourish self-control through the expression and strengthening of appropriate emotional response. Emotionality is a richly human trait which adds considerable meaning to one's existence. Its expression should take place on an enlarged rather than a decreased portion of the spectrum. Of course, the school will help children grow in their capacity to exer-

[3] Arthur T. Jersild, *In Search Of Self*, New York, Bureau of Publications, Columbia University, 1952.

cise restraints; but it will not do so by an image which dries up their emotional response.

The more common meaning of self-control as it applies to schools is the idea of self-rule. Self-control in this sense is practiced in many good elementary schools by allowing children to assume a more active role in developing their own rules of conduct as well as in making the rules work. In the hands of an adequate teacher this is an effective approach. It is good for children to have such involvement and experience in managing their own affairs, for it is in consonance with their way of life. The school which can successfully involve children in such self-rule is demonstrating one of the most significant characteristics of a qualitative approach.

Authority

If this is a world of permissiveness at home, play therapy at school, and self-control in the classroom, where is the provision for the essential authority that is necessary to hold things together? How can parents or teachers control a situation so that the house will be livable, the trip to the museum orderly, and the schoolroom a place in which studying can be done? What can give to the adult voice the note of authority which produces attentive response; the indication that the person will be listened to and if necessary obeyed? This note of authority, says Margaret Mead, is absent from the nagging voice of the Cockney mother, and from the voice of the "enlightened" American father as well. Is it necessary to return to the old authoritarian, fear-enforced, hell and damnation type of control in order to get back the note of authority? Mead says it is not. The note of authority can come back, she says, with a difference. The adult voice can now say implicitly:

I am the person in charge of this situation, the person who will be held responsible if anything goes wrong, the person with the experience, the knowledge (or perhaps just the time) to take charge. I promise not to abuse my authority. But if you are to take part in this situation—at the dinner table, school expedition, picnic—you must obey those orders which I find it necessary to give.[4]

[4] Margaret Mead, "A New Kind of Discipline," *Parents' Magazine,* September, 1959, p. 86.

Mead would have the individual say this without apology, and with full recognition on the part of the adult that obedience is asked not in terms of the divine right of adults, but simply because "I am in charge." And because it is the nature of situations involving children that someone in charge is needed, the person can speak clearly and without hesitation as a good policeman at a street corner, or a fireman at a fire, or the nurse in the doctor's office who says "come this way please." But the other side of the coin, the promise not to abuse the authority, is just as imperative. Policemen do not interrupt the crossing to demand that you take your fingers out of your mouth. The nurse does not interrupt your visit to request that you not hum under your breath. And the fireman does not criticize one's taste in art as he strips the paintings from the wall.

Mead believes that along with our rejection of fear and punishment as part of the adult authority system has also gone a rejection of the all-embracing kind of interference with life which many parents thought was their right:

. . . to put a stop to fidgeting whenever and wherever they found it; to demand attention at every moment no matter how dull their conversation and how exquisite the day-dream on which the child's inner eye was fixed; to invade the child's life under a thousand small pretexts. The new authority note does not go one inch beyond the appropriate situation, . . . but in this one is only extending into the home what has always been an American attitude towards authority in the army and at work—a deep resentment of its exercise outside the proper limits. The revolution in child care in the last twenty-five years has been an attempt to state the limits and the tone of voice appropriate for teacher and parent.[5]

This is Margaret Mead's view of authority, beautifully expressed throughout and as sensible as overshoes on a rainy day; it blows like a breath of fresh air through the psychological fall-out that has invaded the thinking of the present generation of adults. One of the more interesting aspects of this matter is that life as a teacher or parent has become so twisted that it is necessary even to utter such common sense remarks. The interested reader should turn to the complete article for a full expression of her thinking on discipline, for it is both refreshing and helpful. And it is a relief to many adults to have from such a thoughtful observer of the human scene a prac-

[5] *Ibid.*, p. 87.

tical and enlightened delineation of how one may properly assume his adult role in the creation of a healthy discipline. This is surely one of the abiding characteristics of the qualitative school.

Creative Discipline

Freddy was a wholesome and mischievous sixth-grade boy. He was a sort of red-blooded All-American type, who fortunately grace all elementary schools with their presence. The schools are infinitely richer because of the Freddies that roam the world, even though they make it difficult for the classroom to remain in the state of tranquility that most teachers prefer. Freddy had a high compression engine and occasionally, when tranquility had rested on his shoulders for too prolonged a period of time, something would have to give.

Freddy's teacher seemed to understand how it was with boys who had high compression engines, and the two of them enjoyed a sturdy sort of relationship. His teacher had taught him a great deal about athletics and seemed to appreciate the fine qualities of the boy, as well as to realistically accept those that created difficulty. He always seemed to know when pressures were building up in Freddy and when he was about ready to erupt.

One day, the teacher was holding a discussion in social studies. It was a very special discussion in that it was an example of what the teacher had been trying to achieve with the class for some time. The children were staying on the track, and were talking among themselves without the necessity of involving the teacher each time a child spoke. Things were moving along handsomely. At this delicate point in the proceedings, the teacher glanced over at Freddy and recognized the storm warnings. He was not taking part in the discussion and seemed to be on the verge of disrupting what was taking place.

The dilemma that confronted the teacher was simply this: he did not wish to do anything to spoil the kind of a discussion which had been so painstakingly achieved, but he had to prevent Freddy's disturbance before it occurred. On an impulse, he walked over to his desk and quickly wrote the following note:

Dear Freddy,
  Please do not cause me to come to grips with you today.
                                          Sincerely,
                                          Mr. ————————

He then quietly placed the note on Freddy's desk. Freddy unfolded and read the note. He smiled, then shifted unobtrusively into the discussion and helped to move it along. A minor crisis was resolved and the discussion was a success.

The incident above may indicate one of the significant hallmarks of excellent discipline. The approach that was used was tailor-made to the circumstances, to the kind of boy that was involved, and to the kind of a relationship that existed between the child and his teacher. The technique could probably never be used again in quite the same manner with quite the same results, for it was uniquely and creatively derived from the factors present in that particular situation. No teacher could achieve a constant state of discipline this individualized or this creatively derived, but he can implement the degree which he is able to provide. It is a characteristic in discipline which reflects maturity as well as resourcefulness, and it is present to some degree in the discipline of the qualitative school.

Rules

A thoughtful principal of an elementary school found when he assumed the principalship that he had inherited a divided faculty. Two major groups had formed around two of the stronger teachers, and they were almost always at odds with one another. Whatever decisions were to be made were certain to be additionally complicated by this factor; for if one group was for an idea the other would be dynamically opposed.

No doubt the principal aged greatly in his first year, for this condition drains and wastes human energies by wrongfully dissipating them against one another, and it creates such a stalemated condition that any constructive activity is unlikely. In discussing the situation, the principal described a technique which had been beneficial in at least a limited sense. When a problem was before the faculty and the groups were sharply opposed, he would air the differences as fully and as candidly as might be required. He made certain that the differences were adequately represented. Then he would deliberately stop short of bringing the matter to a vote or invoking a rule. Instead he would seek *to substitute understanding for the rule*. He would ask his faculty to deliberate about the matter, and to modify their individual actions to the extent that a rule might be unnecessary. The principal did not make use of his approach as an easy way out, or because he was weak. His faculty knew that if a given situation did not improve satisfactorily there would be a rule, and that it would be enforced. He used the approach because he believed that rules are frequently overdone, that they exist in a given situation to the extent that enlightened behavior does not prevail, and that they are a poor substitute for understanding itself. This is a remarkable and worthy observation of the quality of human relationships, whether within or without the school.

Shifting the consideration now to the elementary classroom, there is reason to believe that teachers might replace *some of the rules* that currently prevail in their classrooms with understanding instead. Perhaps only the unusual teacher could make it work, but this is to be expected—unusual teachers and qualitative practices enjoy the closest of kinships. Bit by bit, and brick by brick, such a process contributes to the maturing of the child and his progressive march toward independence. It is a worthy goal which seems to justify the time and resourcefulness required to achieve it, for it is an accomplishment of character rather than of conduct. Lao Tze said it best in the following beautiful and provocative remarks:

> . . . After Nature was lost, one talked of character:
> After character was lost, one talked of kindness:
> After kindness was lost, one talked of righteousness:
> After righteousness was lost, one talked of rules of conduct:
> Now, rules of conduct indicate the thinning out of the innate honesty of man.

Summary

Discipline has been interpreted as one of the major concerns of our time. A healthy and constructive approach to discipline is an achievement of the first magnitude, and requires the best efforts of all concerned. Some of the attitudes and recommendations on discipline today do not seem to be thoughtfully derived. They are horseback estimates of the situation, based on a superficial assessment of the problem and a lack of insight into the job to be done. Thus, permissiveness has been widely discredited and maligned even though it is an essential element of the kind of development that is being sought.

Discipline is essentially a personal matter, and parents and teachers must invoke practices which best reflect their own inner convictions. Whatever decisions are made, however, should be based not only on what one believes to be right, but also on the image of *what he wishes the child to become.* With this in mind, it has been suggested that a qualitative approach to discipline is one which:

1. *Retains an enlightened permissiveness* at home and at school.
2. Strives for a *healthy form* of self-control.
3. Operates sensitively within *the proper limits* of adult authority.
4. Adjusts its practices *creatively* to the circumstances and to the child.
5. Moves deliberately forward in the substitution of *understanding for rules.*

Chapter 10

Grouping

Grouping is a very controversial matter, and many segments of the profession are in honest disagreement about how this important function should be performed. One reason for the continuing controversy is that the problem has been underestimated. It is just as difficult to approach perfection in grouping children for maximum learning as it is to approach perfection in science or any other area of the curriculum. This complexity is rarely recognized, however, and much less time is devoted to perfecting the system than to improving some segment such as the reading program. Yet, grouping is a pervading curriculum matter which reaches across subject boundaries, and influences success in reading, science, and many other aspects of the program. Grouping cannot be regarded casually in a school which is striving for excellence, and it cannot be resolved by some of the naïve questions that are heatedly debated today. The question of which is better, homogeneous or heterogeneous grouping, is not an answerable question. It is like raising the question of which is better, a dentist or an obstetrician.

The curricular function of grouping is to place a child in the human environment in which he can learn best and learn most. Such a problem has three principal phases. The first phase is the initial assigning of a group of children to a teacher. This is an administrative function which is usually referred to as classification. In the second phase, the teacher groups children within her room in an effort to individualize the learning. This is known as internal grouping. In the third phase, at the end of a given period of time, children are traditionally regrouped or reassigned for the next year's work. This is called promotion. All three phases are a part of the concept of grouping, for children are grouped in classifying them, grouped within the room for purposes of instruction, and grouped again for continuation of learning. Learning may be influenced by the decisions that are made in any of the three phases, and the central task is that of placing and maintaining a child in that group in which his growth may take place most effectively.

This discussion points up some of the dimensions of the problem by suggesting six points at which the process can be improved. There are additional ways to effect improvement, but a school which can successfully implement these six proposals should have little difficulty with the others. Not a single one of the proposals is easily accomplished. Furthermore, not a single one of them can be implemented and then forgotten; for grouping, like discipline, is a dynamic matter that requires continuing attention and adjustment. It calls for the kind of alertness, analysis, and manipulation that one observes in a superbly coached team. The function can never be successfully mechanized, nor can it be properly bottled and shelved. Perhaps this is one of the reasons why grouping in so many schools operates at a low level of quality. It may also be, at the same time, a motivation for striving to see that the condition is improved.

Flexible Admissions

One of the first points at which a school can demonstrate quality in its grouping practices is in its admission policy. This policy should be more flexibly adjusted to allow maturity to be a factor in admission, in addition to mere chronological age. At the present time, in almost all school districts throughout the United States, children are admitted to school on the basis of chronological age. Thus, a child may enter first grade if he is six years of age on or before a specified date. The date is usually set by the school district itself. If a child in a given district is allowed to enter first grade by virtue of being six years of age on or before December 1st, he might begin his first grade experience at the calendar or chronological age of five years and nine months. The specified date is sometimes later than December 1st, in which case the child is allowed to enter at an even earlier age than five years and nine months. If the date is earlier than December 1st, the effect is to cause him to enroll at an age correspondingly later than the five years and nine months.

Chronological age is an uncomplicated and useful admission device and is typically regarded as the most important single criterion for grouping. It becomes questionable as a practice when it is used as the only criterion for admission, for it cannot adequately do the job alone. This becomes obvious when one considers the following:

School X allows children who will be six years old on or before December 1st to enter first grade in September. Child A is relatively immature and has a birthday November 30. In terms of total growth or organismic age, Child A in September approximates the level of development which is typical of an average five year old. Child A, however, by application of a single criterion of chronological age will be admitted to first grade.

Child B has a birthday on December the 2nd. In terms of total growth Child B is advanced in many aspects of his development and roughly approximates the maturity level of an average six year old child. Chronologically he is three days younger than Child A, but with respect to maturity he is a year more advanced. Child B is ready to profit from a first grade experience, but under the application of a single criterion of admission such as chronological age, he would not be allowed to enter school.

A flexible admission policy would allow the level of maturity of a child to become a factor in the decision as to when he might enter school. It would not replace the criterion of chronological age, but would supplement it, and realistically improve the conditions for entering school. Some observers say such a practice is not administratively feasible. This has never been demonstrated and is an evasion of the problem. If the practice is worthwhile, creative administrators will find ways to implement it. The function of administration is to serve and facilitate the growth of desirable curriculum practices rather than to prevent them from taking place. The qualitative school will find ways to introduce this kind of flexibility into its admission policy, and will allow the maturity of the child to become a factor in whatever decision is to be made.

Nongraded Schools

In recent times, an increasing number of enlightened schools have become aware of the inadequacies of classifying children by grades. Graded-school organization introduces a rigidity into the classification of children that hinders its effectiveness, for once the child's classification is made it becomes relatively fixed. Even though his growth pattern and other relevant circumstances may indicate later that he is improperly placed, it becomes extremely difficult to make a proper adjustment. Once the grade lines are drawn they are not easily crossed, for they carry emotional connotations as well as elements of status and prestige. The result, of course, is that a change in the child's grade level, or vertical position in the program, tends to be avoided. This thwarts the essential purpose of grouping, for a proper vertical alignment is intimately related to the central task of placing him in a human environment in which he can learn most effectively.

There is, additionally, a great lack of realism in the concept of the graded school due simply to the facts of individual differences. The wise teacher knows that his children do not fit the grade they are in. In fact, if one beams fifth grade material at a typical fifth grade class he will *miss most of the students.* This is because the number functioning below a fifth grade level plus the number functioning above it exceeds the number to whom it is properly directed. Thus, the more advanced elementary schools have sought to find a better way, and have experimented with the idea of the nongraded school.

One form of the nongraded school is known as the Primary-Intermediate Plan. This is an organizational arrangement that seeks to remove some of the rigidities of the graded school, and classifies children by divisions rather than by grades. Thus, a child enters school at the age of six and is assigned to the primary department with other six year olds. He is not in first grade, for there is no first grade. His room may be designated as the John Glenn Room, or as the six year olds, or any other neutral designation.

The teacher in charge of the "sixes" would be counseled somewhat as follows:

Here are your thirty-five children. They are all six but they are all different. Your job is simply to accept them as they are, and take them as far as they can go. There are no fixed expectations as to how much they are to accomplish. Please avoid pressuring them to do tasks which they are not ready to undertake, but allow them equal opportunity to learn. Help each of them to grow in terms of his individual capacity to achieve. Whether it is large or small, the amount of growth desired from the class is that amount that is appropriate for this group of six year olds.

Thus freed from formal expectations of a predetermined and fixed amount of content to be covered, or growth to be achieved, the teacher of the sixes is thought to be in a position to be more responsive to children's needs. He is free to create a learning environment that is just right for them. The children automatically become seven after a year of being six, and the teacher of the sevens is specifically instructed to pick them up where they left off and carry on from there.

After three years in the primary department, the school usually sets up a sort of check station for determining whether or not the child is ready to go on to the intermediate department. If, in the judgment of the teacher, the child is not ready for the more advanced work of the intermediate department, he may be held back for one or even two semesters of work. There is a careful avoidance of the word failure at this point. The child and his parents are told that he simply has not completed his work. Presumably, the child may advance flexibly into the intermediate department whenever his work has been completed. If it requires the full two semesters to do the job, he has spent an additional year in the primary division and is then ten years old.

The machinery in the intermediate division operates in the same fashion. The child who has spent an extra year in the primary division would be ten, eleven, and twelve during his three years in the intermediate department. A similar check station functions in the third year of the intermediate division, and he might be held up for as much as another full year here before advancing to the junior high school. As indicated in Figure 1, all children are to be moved out of the elementary school at the age of thirteen on the assumption that their developmental characteristics make it inappropriate for them to be any longer a part of the elementary school.

Five advantages are ordinarily claimed by those who favor the Primary-Intermediate Plan:

1. It reduces failure. This is true in a quantitative sense at least, for it may happen only at two points rather than at six. Obviously, however, removing the language of failure is not the equivalent of removing failure itself.

FIGURE 1

The Graded Plan			The Primary–Intermediate Plan		
CL	Age	P. A.	CL	AGE	P. A.
6	11	16–17		Check Station	13
				. . . .	
5	10	14–15		11	12
			I	10	11
4	9	12–13		9	10
3	8	10–11		Check Station	9
				. . . .	
2	7	8–9		8	
			P	7	
1	6	6–7		6	
Emphasizes:			Emphasizes:		
Standards			Growth Patterns		
Continuity of Teaching			Continuity of Learning		
Minimum Goals			Child Development		

LEGEND: CL–Classification P. A.–Possible Age P–Primary I–Intermediate

2. *It promotes continuity in learning.* There is some support for this claim in the sense that teachers are freed from the pressure of bringing all their children to a given point. The facts of human differences are more realistically accepted, and teachers are thus in a position to adjust the curriculum to the group. There is, of course, no assurance that this will be done.

3. *It promotes pupil security.* This may be true in the sense that a child is not confronted with the yearly threat of being separated from his group. He becomes a member of a group and enjoys the security of remaining a part of it for at least three years.

4. *It is more compatible with known facts of child development.* There is some substance to this claim. Plateaus in learning are common to all children. They may be caused by shock, illness, injury, or simply by the process of catching up with oneself. If a child hits a plateau during a given year, and remains on the plateau for a substantial portion of the year, he may be doomed to failure. The wider division of time in the Primary-Intermediate Plan allows for both the plateau and the growth spurt which follows. This may allow a child to regain the growth which was lost for circumstances

over which he had no control, and to catch up with his group without ever being retained.

5. *It is more flexible in operation.* There is a definite possibility of more flexibility. As was pointed out earlier, the presence of grades stratifies the organization and tends to make a more rigid structure. The ungraded school has as much freedom of maneuver horizontally and more freedom vertically.

Although there are difficulties in implementing the concept of the nongraded school, the basic idea is sufficiently promising to warrant the attempt. The idea is more easily implemented in the primary grades where the content burden of the curriculum is less heavy and there is more freedom to attempt innovations. Thus, the child's first placement in school should be in a "gray zone" that is deliberately unclassified as to grade level. The curriculum of this unclassified division might correspond roughly to that of kindergarten, first, and second grades, representing a three-year block. Emphasis in this division should be upon careful observation and study of the children, provision for extension and enrichment of their firsthand experiences, and the initial development of language, social, and number tools. The more slowly developing children might take three full years in this division. Normal children moving along at a more adequate pace might spend two years in the ungraded primary, and gifted children might complete it in one. The ungraded aspect of this segment of the school permits greater flexibility in adjusting rates of progress to the maturity of the child, and allows vertical acceleration or slowing down to proceed with less difficulty. Such an innovation, even if it is limited to the primary grades, moves closer to the ideal of an excellent approach.

Planned Diversity in Grouping

The vision of a strong, new nation as a vast melting pot was part of the Great American Dream. This vision can function in a small way in every classroom in the country. It is fostered by deliberately building certain kinds of differences into the composition of each class. Such differences are then the product of design rather than of accident.

Building this element of quality into the school's grouping practices operates in the following manner. The principal and the teachers who are to receive the children sit around a table together. Using their combined information about the children, they form groups which contain the kinds of differences they wish to include. Thus, each teacher will receive her share of the rich and the poor, the aggressive and the shy, the boys and the girls, the leaders and the followers, etc. The inclusion of such differences in the composition of each classroom is not left to chance as is done in most schools. Each room, instead, is deliberately shaped in the image of the great original dream.

The forming of such heterogeneous groups, however, can be simultaneously controlled with respect to the vertical spread or levels of achievement and ability. Achievement levels in a typical classroom often span six or more grades. Most teachers feel that this unnecessarily complicates their job, and that the spread is an important factor in teacher load. Rightly or wrongly, teachers feel they can work more easily and effectively with a group of children which spans three grade levels of achievement than with one which spans six.

The vertical spread of achievement can be a conscious part of the formation of each group. At the same time that sociological heterogeneity is being built into the groups, vertical levels of achievement or ability can be reduced. For example, one-hundred-fifty fifth graders might typically represent a spread of achievement from first grade to ninth. No teacher, however, needs to have the complete range of achievement in her room in order to have the kinds of differences that are desired. The formation of any given class can be deliberately formed with respect to controlling this range. Each teacher's group can be restricted to any three contiguous levels of ability or achievement in order to be sensitive to the factor of teaching load.

Such a proposal is in sharp contrast to the debate of homogeneous versus heterogeneous grouping, for some kinds of difference in the classrooms are obviously desirable, and others should obviously be controlled. This is a way to draw from the intrinsic strengths of both homogeneity and heterogeneity. It is a concept and a procedure which can help to reconcile divergent views, for in a highly significant way it is sensitive to the merits of each. Classification on such a basis seems vastly improved.

Balanced Internal Groupings

The discussion up to this point has been concerned with the improvement of grouping through more realistic admission practices, more flexible types of gross organization as exemplified in the nongraded school, and a more carefully diversified composition of the class each teacher is to receive. At this stage, the teacher ordinarily forms some kind of internal groupings in his own room in order to further individualize the instruction. The most common example of such internal grouping is in the reading program. Here, the teacher traditionally forms the best, middle, and slowest groups in a sincere attempt to adjust the program to each child.

Balanced internal grouping is a qualitative factor which should be invoked if a practice such as the three reading groups prevails in a given classroom. As indicated in the previous discussion of the teaching of reading, children in the lower groups tend to get farther and farther behind, and more and more discouraged.[1] This has been interpreted as being of major significance because it is tampering with the child's self-concept. It is of great importance for every child to believe that he is indeed a worthy self, and the school should consciously reinforce this view.

When a teacher, therefore, sets up such status groupings in his room, he has an obligation at the same time to set up the antidote. This is accomplished by arranging groupings in other parts of the curriculum in which a child who has been cast in an inferior role in one aspect of the program may have a chance to lead or excel in another. This is a simple compensating factor, but it is an act of fair play and justice as well.

Such groupings do not need to be balanced on a one to one basis. The point is that no one can afford to be cast constantly in an inferior role, and an occasional situation in which one can achieve recognition and respect may be all that is necessary. Some of the more thoughtful elementary teachers have a bit of philosophy related to this. They believe that every child in their room has a special gift, and it is their job to discover it. When each child's gift is discovered and recognized, the essential purpose of balanced internal groupings is accomplished. It is probably accurate to suggest

[1] See Chapter 6, p. 75.

that not enough of the nation's elementary teachers have recognized and shouldered this particular professional obligation. It is a sensitivity, however, which is a vital part of an excellent approach.

Personal Needs Grouping

Martha was a fifth grade girl who seemed always to be on the outside looking in. In any kind of a game or activity in which the children would choose teams, she would invariably be the last one to be chosen. She was shunned in committee work, shunned on the playground, and she even walked to and from school alone. She was very hungry for friends and tried ever so hard to be a part of other children's lives, but no one would let her in.

Her teacher was aware of Martha's hunger for companionship and acceptance, and he made discreet efforts of his own to see that she was included in the affairs of the class. After three months of the school year he could not see that he had made any headway, however, in making her an accepted member of the class. One evening, he asked three of the most popular members of the class to stay after school, and laid the problem in their laps. He told them how lonely Martha was, how she longed to have friends and to be a part of the children's lives, and how he had been unable to help her become a really accepted member of the group.

The children, of course, rose to the occasion and said all of the right things. They would see that she was chosen for committees in the classroom. They would see that she was included in their games on the playground. They would see that she did not have to walk to school alone.

There are many children in the elementary schools who long to be on the inside of a small circle of friends, but seem to have no way of getting there. They are like a "have-not" child at the Christmas season with his nose pressed against the display windows wistfully contemplating the beauty inside. The world is full of children like Martha who are always on the outside looking in. They have a deep hunger for responsiveness and human companionship. If their hunger is not alleviated in some way their lives will become further twisted, and for them as well as for the world in which they are to live the effect is detrimental.

Personal needs grouping is a concept which *recognizes the personal hungers of children, and tries to be responsive to them.* It attempts to set up grouping arrangements in which the isolates can work with the stars. Perhaps the activity which is used to bring them together is a simple and transitory one like the arranging of a bulletin board. But the children are deliberately brought together *under circumstances which are as favorable as possible to the have-not child.* This aspect of grouping is largely unused, and a surprising number of teachers have never even considered the idea. In the hands of master teachers such a concept can make the classroom a better and happier place for many children in the elementary school. It can even help to make the world a better place to live. It adds a touch of excellence which no school can afford to ignore.

Flexible Regrouping

Stanley's father brought the family out of the hills of Kentucky and moved to a city in Eastern Indiana. The next morning Stanley went to enroll in school. He was ten years old and had never been to school a day in his life. He strode eagerly in to the principal's office to tell him of his desire to matriculate, and the principal looked at him in frank wonderment. He was barefooted, his clean but frayed trousers hung just below the knees, and he was absolutely delighted to be embarking upon his education. The principal had never seen one like this—he was like a young Abraham Lincoln.

Perplexed over where he should place the boy, he called in his primary teachers and put the problem up to them. They, too, were perplexed, and finally had to leave for their classes without making a recommendation. Still in a quandry on the matter, the principal called the boy back into his office. Stanley must have heard the conversations about him, for he said something to the principal which the man will never forget. ". . . Mr. Moore, I don't care where you place me, but I just want to learn to read."

Mr. Moore was very impressed with the boy and worked out a special arrangement for him. Stanley was to go to the first grade until he had learned to read. When this was accomplished he would be moved to the second grade, and when he had mastered what was being done in the second grade, he would be advanced to the third. He could move as rapidly as he was able to master the program. Stanley liked this idea and said he would also help the teacher.

Stanley liked the idea so much that he arrived at school the next morning at 5:30. No one was there but the custodian. He looked around at the empty halls and classrooms and asked the custodian, "Where are all the scholars?"

When the others arrived at 8:30, Stanley took his place with the six year olds. He towered over them like a giant sequoia, but he was helpful to the teacher and he learned rapidly. In four weeks he mastered the work and was ready to move on to the second grade. It was such a happy event that the school had a simple graduation ceremony for him. He mastered second grade in six weeks and moved into the third. By the end of the semester he was in fourth grade where he finished the year. He was the most popular and respected boy in the school.

Near the end of the year Stanley's father moved the family back into the hills of Kentucky. Every adult in the school who had worked with Stanley wept unashamedly. None of them know what became of him. It would be pleasant to think that someday he might be President of the United States of America. He has had five votes pledged to him since 1949 if he ever wishes to use them.

It was stated in the introductory remarks that the essential purpose of grouping is to place a child in the human environment in which he could learn best and learn most. Flexible regrouping is a concept which is necessary in order to keep abreast of the process. Sometimes a child experiences a surge of growth which places him too far beyond his classmates. Suddenly he doesn't fit there any more. He has outgrown them, just as Stanley had outgrown his trousers. Such development will not constrain or relate itself to the school calendar. When, because of such a forward thrust, a child has outgrown the environment in which he was placed, regrouping is in order at that moment instead of waiting for some predetermined point in the school year. Such a thrust of development can occasionally be provided for through the internal groupings within the room. The concept of flexible regrouping requires opening the door for the crossing of grade lines, also, whenever the case warrants doing so. Grade lines, if they must be maintained in a given school, are not sacred. They can be crossed at will whenever an imaginative and resourceful school wishes to cross them. This is an additional characteristic of the grouping in a qualitative school.

Summary

Grouping has been interpreted as one of the most important aspects of the elementary program. It has a pervading function in the sense that it crosses subject boundaries, and influences children's attitudes and success in many portions of their total school experience. Its special curricular role is that of placing and maintaining a child in the human environment in which his development may proceed most effectively.

It is doubtful that many schools have recognized the real significance of this problem, and the dimensions that are involved if a school genuinely seeks excellence in its approach. Many schools still function at the level of debating the misconceived issue of homogenous versus heterogeneous grouping. Such a debate indicates that the problem is not seen in its larger context.

The larger context involves the thoughtful identification of major points at which grouping impinges upon and significantly influences learning. Six of these points have been interpreted as being of considerable importance. Thus, a qualitative approach to grouping is one which:

1. Uses maturity as a factor in admission in addition to mere chronological age.
2. Implements a nongraded form of school organization at least in the primary grades.
3. Builds diversity with a controlled vertical range deliberately into the composition of each class.
4. Balances any ability groupings to be used with the recognized antidote of success.
5. Forms additional groupings specifically designed for the personality needs of children.
6. Bases the regrouping of children on patterns of growth instead of the school calendar.

Chapter 11

Evaluating and Reporting Progress

There are probably three assumptions implicit in the general process of marking and reporting: (1) the school, being a specialized environment for learning, produces results in the form of individual growth and achievement, (2) it is desirable to determine with some specificity what individual growth and achievement is transpiring, and (3) reporting this information to the affected parties is desirable and conducive to further learning. The heart of the matter would seem to be that of linking the practices as directly and specifically as possible to the growth process. Thus, the key criterion in determining whether or not a given practice in marking and reporting is desirable is simply whether or not it provides information which furthers in any important way the progress and development of the child. Simple and fundamental as this criterion may be, it has not always been the prevailing factor upon which decisions were made.

The chief methods of evaluating and reporting progress seem to be embodied in a relatively small number of types, and an examination of these may help to develop some degree of perspective on the matter. Such a review may be helpful, also, in pointing up clues to some of the more qualitative factors in this aspect of the curriculum.

The Percentage Method. This method graded a child on the basis of one-hundred being a possible and perfect score. Thus, a child might get 85 in arithmetic, 90 in geography and 99 in health. Relatively few schools use this method today. Some felt it an act of hypocrisy to pretend that they could appraise with such accuracy that there was a discernible difference, for example, between a 74 and a 75. Others felt that it was impossible to compare and equate a score in one area of the curriculum with that of another. For instance, is an 85 in arithmetic comparable to an 85 in creative art? Some pointed out that the act of quantification was in itself out of line with major purposes of the curriculum. That is to say that the curriculum was seeking to further personal development, and many forms of desired growth could not presently be quantified even if it could be established as desirable to do so. The criticism and objections were sufficiently strong to give rise to a different technique, and many schools seemed to move toward the five-point scale.

The Scale Technique. In this technique, there was a tendency to use grades such as A, B, C, D, E. The grades were competitively derived and were to be based on what was known as the normal curve. The largest number of students (approximately two-thirds of a given group) were to receive the C, or average grade. The grade B represented work that was definitely above average. Approximately the same number of students that received a B were also to receive a D, which was the grade representing work definitely below average. The distinctly superior grade was A, and the failing grade was E, with again an approximately equal number of students to receive the highest and the lowest grade.

A major criticism of the scale method centered around the obscurities upon which it was based. What did the grade mean? Was it, for instance, based upon achievement, or effort, or attitude, or growth, or some combination thereof? This controversy was never adequately resolved. Therefore, the A did not mean the same thing from school to school nor from teacher to teacher. There is even considerable reason to believe that A's given by the same person do not have similar meanings. This weakness is an inherent aspect of the technique, for the letter grade is simply a symbol of the multiple aspects of achievement which it hopes to represent but cannot adequately convey. Too much meaning has been packed into the symbols. Grouping multiple meanings, and attempting to interpret them by symbols, causes a loss of identities. The meanings are thus jumbled together, blurred, averaged, and obscured. The symbol is glorified, and meanings as they relate to any specific or significant aspects of the child's personality and growth are lost in the process. No one knows, when he looks at a letter grade, what it tells about a particular child that will be valuable in furthering his development; but more curiously, so few seem to care. One of the anomalies of the current educational scene is the degree to which parents uncritically accept a reporting device which does not report. One can only conclude that this is an area of the curriculum in which an impressive number of people are uninformed.

The Modified Scale. Some of the schools that abandoned the five-point scale changed to a modified version in the form of plus ($+$), check ($\sqrt{}$), and minus ($-$). A plus ordinarily indicated very satisfactory work, a check meant that the work was passing but needed to be improved, and a minus was given for work that was unsatisfactory. There were many variations of the plan. One variation that was commonly used was the S, I, and U. S indicated work that was satisfactory, I indicated the need for improvement, and U meant unsatisfactory or failing work.

The modified scale represented a big point of departure from the scale *in the sense that the grades were not competitively derived.* Under this plan, children tended to be graded in terms of their ability to perform. Thus, no matter how little a child learned he was given a satisfactory mark if he had done as well as he could do. On the other hand, a child whose ability was greater and who was not achieving as much as he could, might receive an I or U.

This was difficult for parents to understand, for under such a system it was possible for a slow child working up to ability to receive S for each grading period throughout the year and still fail the grade. Conversely, it was possible for a bright child working beneath his level of ability to receive unsatisfactory marks each grading period and still be promoted. Something was obviously wrong with the communication. The evaluative symbols did not mean what the recipients thought they meant. The reporting device was again failing to report.

The Narrative Report. One of the more recent forms of reporting to parents is the narrative report. With this method, the teacher has an opportunity to write an intimate and personalized account of the child's growth. He is free to select and interpret any information which would be constructive and helpful in furthering the education of the child. Both positive and negative factors may be woven into the account. Items of information appearing in the report are chosen by virtue of being true, being important or significant with respect to interpreting the stage of development of a particular child, and being useful to the parents in increasing their understanding of the child's progress as well as their own role in facilitating the process. The report usually begins and ends on a positive note. It attempts, within the bounds of professional discretion, to provide the *kinds of information parents want to know*. It may indicate specific ways in which the child can improve, and specific ways in which the parents may assist in the undertaking. The method is directly keyed to the factor of child growth, and to the basic function which marking and reporting as an aspect of the curriculum should serve. It is dynamic enough as a practice to be as effective as the person using it. Its potentiality is limited only by the understanding and skill of teachers themselves. In the hands of a person who has a deep understanding of his children and the power to communicate his thoughts, it can be a highly personalized and extremely effective reporting device.

Some critics say of the narrative report that it is too time consuming to be practical. This claim has no merit. Anyone who can organize and write down his thoughts can develop the report as quickly and easily as he can average out and arrive at letter grades. Even if it required more time, however, it would be considerably better to have one good report each semester than two or three inferior ones. Others say that teachers cannot write well enough to use the narrative report. This statement is too incredible to dignify with an answer. Still others say that the teacher does not know enough about his individual children to write a report about them as individuals. It is true that if one has no information to communicate, then a method of communication is unnecessary. Any teacher whose thoughts are that barren should be excused not only from writing the report, but from the pretense of being a teacher as well.

The Planned-Parent Conference. The planned-parent conference is similar in philosophy and intent to the narrative report, but sets out to do the job in a face-to-face relationship rather than by note-writing. Such a conference is usually scheduled in advance so that the parent as well as the teacher may plan for it. A half-hour is ordinarily set aside in order that it may proceed in an unhurried atmosphere, and classes may be dismissed in order that the job can be given priority attention. The teacher has actual specimens of the child's work to be discussed with the parents, and the well-handled conference becomes a reciprocal process, with the teacher receiving as well as giving valuable information relative to the child.

The planned-parent conference has certain inherent advantages over the narrative report. A face-to-face relationship makes possible a spirit and degree of cooperation that can hardly be engendered in any other way. *Furthermore, the understandings can go beyond what were held by either party prior to the conference, for the discussion may provide new clues and stimulate ideas and insights which did not exist before the conference was held.* In addition, there is a communication advantage. Concrete evidence of the child's work offers one communication advantage. Another is afforded by the give-and-take of discussion, which enables a perceptive teacher to reinterpret and reemphasize an idea that may not be clearly understood, to answer questions stimulated by the information, and to otherwise more nearly create the exact shades of understanding desired.

The Concept of Essential Functions. This concept is similar to the approach used in identifying elements of quality in grouping. It seeks to rise above the debate of a specific issue such as competitive grading and to delineate the major functions to be performed by this aspect of the program. Seven essential functions are interpreted as being necessary in order to perform the role that evaluating and reporting is designed to perform. These seven essential functions constitute a powerful set of criteria. If the system used by a given school is adequately performing each of the seven it has achieved a marked degree of excellence in its approach. Each of the functions will be described and interpreted in the discussion which follows.

The Information Function

The system, whatever its form, should stress the kinds of information about children that parents want to know. Obviously, the information should be within the bounds of professional discretion, and should be selected so as to be helpful rather than harmful. The parent, however, needs and deserves to be informed about many aspects of his child's work. Being informed means being in a position to help the school maximize its influence. It makes the essential relationship between schools and parents a more effective partnership. The reporting system might reasonably include information such as the following:

1. The child's work habits.
2. His relationships with others.
3. His personal strengths.
4. His specific progress.
5. His level of academic attainment.
6. His present deficiencies.
7. The reasons for his deficiencies.
8. The degree to which he can be expected to improve.
9. The ways in which the parents can help.

This aspect of the reporting system would be strengthened by working directly with parents to more realistically determine what they wish to know. Such information is not conveyed in reporting systems which use the percentage method, the scale method, or the modified scale. *Any information desired, however, can be reflected in either the narrative report or the planned-parent conference.*

The Individualization Function

The system, whatever its form, should lend itself to the description and interpretation of a unique human being. The uniqueness of human personality is largely an unchallenged concept. Almost everyone accepts the fact that this child who is being reported upon is like no other person in the world. A report on the child, therefore, should reflect his uniqueness. It should direct itself specifically and personally to his individuality, and portray it as it is revealed in his school. *It should strive to be genuine and present the truth.* It should portray weaknesses as well as strengths. It should present growth as well as barriers to growth—and all of this should be developed in an individual setting *so that it is about this child that the report speaks and no other.* Consider the following descriptive report on a fifth grade girl:

Nancy is one of the best students I have ever had. On her recent achievement tests she scored at the eighth grade level. One of the unusual aspects of her achievement is that it is so well-rounded. She is performing well above grade level in all of her subjects, and yet, she has time to enter and enjoy all of our extra class activities. She seems well-organized in her study time. She has strong powers of concentration on whatever she undertakes. She thinks unusually well for a ten year old girl, and her ideas are likely to be original and imaginative.

She is extremely well-liked by her classmates. This is partially because she is thoughtful and considerate of others, and partially because she has won their respect. She never pushes herself forward. She seems to have a very wholesome and positive attitude toward school, and toward life. She is a cooperative child, and a tremendous asset to our room.

The school could use a report card that informed Nancy's parents she had made A's in all of her subjects and an A in conduct, but the personal qualities of Nancy as a unique and distinctive child would be lost in the process.

The Self-Evaluation Function

A reporting system, whatever its form, should make some provision for each child's evaluation of himself. Some teachers handle this by holding personal conferences with each child prior to the teacher's conference with the parents. This conference is planned with the children in advance so that they may consciously work toward it and prepare for it. As a result of such planning, they may keep samples of their own work and records of their progress. They may even keep a notebook in which they jot down ideas they want to remember for use in the conference.

Each child may have five minutes to talk privately with his teacher about his own work. He suggests ideas which he feels should be brought to the attention of his parents at the time of their conference. He tells what progress he feels he has made since the last report. He makes suggestions about specimens of his work which can be shown to his parents, and he may suggest also his plans for further improvement.

This can be a very rich experience for a child, and a powerful means of motivation. It encourages pupil responsibility, and heightens his awareness of the purposes of school and his progress and shortcomings in relation to those purposes. Often it produces a desire in children to make better use of their school time. It is also a rich source of information to the teacher. She has a golden opportunity to look inside the child at such moments and to better understand his standards, his anxieties, and his concept of himself. In addition, it tends to draw a child and his teacher closer together in the undertaking of a common task.

The Communication Function

The system, whatever its form, should be able to *communicate* the desired information to the parents concerned. This means that the information must actually *be conveyed*. Such information cannot be conveyed by percentages, or by letter grades. A few parents may actually want to know *only* how their child has performed in competition with other children, and may think that the percentage or letter grade method can do the job. This, however, is rarely the case, for very few teachers grade alike. Strang has indicated this marking variance in her reference to a study conducted by the NEA.[1] In this study, the same arithmetic paper was given to 111 different teachers to grade. The scores given to the paper, however, ranged all the way from 21 to 88. Even on such a narrow and limited responsibility as stating the relative standing of a child, percentages and letter grades are inadequate. Most parents want to know more than that, and a descriptive report or a conference approach *can interpret whatever it is desirable and possible for them to know*. If a fourth grade child is the poorest reader in her class, information such as the following may need to be given to the parents:

Sharon is reading at second grade level. She cannot yet independently master new words, and seems tense and overanxious in the reading lessons. At the present time we are giving her a rather simple and interesting type of story content, and are attempting to build up her word attack skills. She is just now beginning to relax and show some confidence in her work. *It is extremely important to avoid pressuring her, or criticizing her about her reading at this time.*

The above information needs to be communicated, for it may make an important difference in what happens to the child. Such information *can be transmitted,* however, only in a school which uses one of the more personalized types of report.

[1] Ruth Strang, *How to Report Pupil Progress,* Chicago, Science Research Associates, 1955, p. 4.

The Cooperative-Action Function

The results of the evaluation and reporting of progress should lead to additional constructive action. Out of the conference with the child, and the subsequent session with his parents, there should be ideas which can be used to improve the quality of a child's experiences. Some leads will come from the child himself in his preconference. These ideas should be honored if at all possible. They are the seeds of a developing sense of self-direction, to which the curriculum should give a constant priority emphasis. Some of the leads will also grow out of the parent conference. As indicated earlier, one of the unique strengths of the parent conference is that it may generate ideas and insights which neither the parent or the teacher had before the conference was held. The teacher is then in a position to put the pieces together, and to coordinate the efforts of all concerned. The proposed action may be quite simple, such as the temporary removal of pressure; or more involved, such as the change of teachers and rooms. Simple or complex, however, the action is keyed to the basic notion of improving for a given child the quality of his learning environment.

The Fair Play Function

The reporting system should be one in which every child has an approximately equal chance to succeed. Children are captives in the elementary school. They have no choice as to whether or not they come to school; they are forced to attend. Even though they do not go by choice, many of them have a fine attitude toward school and do their very best to succeed. There are still many schools, however, that fail children who do their very best because their best is not good enough. This is very unjust. If children are forced to attend a school which sets standards they cannot possibly reach, it is morally wrong to fail them because they did not succeed. If in a professional school of medicine or law the instructors wish to set standards which many students cannot reach, that is a different matter. No one is required to be a physician or a lawyer. Such students are there by choice and can leave in the same manner. The elementary child, however, has no such choice. His environment is by necessity a specially designed and protected environment. The society which forces him to spend his formative years in such an environment has an obligation to create the environment in such a way that his efforts can produce success. *His best should always be good enough, and it is a mark of ignorance and brutality to have it otherwise.* Both the percentage method and the scale method condone such brutality; neither the narrative report or the planned-parent conference allow it to occur.

Perhaps much of the cruelty that takes place in this regard is thoughtless rather than deliberate. The American citizen has an almost innate passion for justice. He is quick to sense unfairness, and is always rooting for the underdog regardless of how mangy and undeserving it may be. Yet, he is likely not only to accept but to approve letter grades which reward the "haves" and degrade the "have-nots." He would not tolerate a track event in which the swiftest runners were moved up closer to the tape, and the slower runners were moved farther back. This he would recognize as a preposterous arrangement. Yet, he tolerates it every day in the schools, for the informed teacher knows that some children are at the A level of achievement in a subject before the instruction even begins. Others are so far back in achievement in the subject that even though they progress faster than their more favored friends they will still get a poorer grade. Fair play can be reflected in the report only by being sensitive to such factors as (1) background, (2) starting point, (3) native endowment, and (4) achievement in relation to ability to achieve. The older systems of evaluating and reporting are not designed to make allowance for such considerations. Only in the narrative or conference approach is there sufficient opportunity to exercise the function of fair play.

Some will say that the idea under discussion is too soft and unrealistic. Many believe that failure is good for children, and that it helps mature them so that they may grow into seasoned adults. This is partially true. Failure *can be a seasoning or maturing experience* and should not be eliminated from the elementary school. The nature of the elementary school is such, however, that failure should occur *only under circumstances over which it is possible for the child to exercise control.* If he can do it and doesn't, then failure may properly and justly apply. To fail a child, however, for not achieving a task which is impossible for him to achieve is detrimental. Such failure is not realistic, and instead of maturing a child it causes him to harden and withdraw. He learns to dislike learning, and a mortal blow has been struck at his desire as well as his capacity to grow. That is why the fair play function must find expression in any system striving to achieve an excellent approach.

The Standards Function

A system of marking and reporting should reflect and maintain the high standards of the school. Many sincere patrons of the school would be disturbed about the philosophy which was enunciated about fair play in the preceding discussion. They feel that accepting achievement which is relatively low, simply because it is the best one can do, will lower standards and detract from the quality of the program. This is a thoughtful observation and a legitimate concern. Standards are levels of expectation or achievement indicating degrees of acceptability or excellence. Will they be harmed or strengthened by the fair play concept?

The essential meaning of the fair play concept is that no one should be expected or required to do more than he can do. Conversely, it is legitimate within the fair play concept to expect and require students to do as well as they can. This is precisely the point at which the concept of standards moves in. If the children in a given school are doing as well as they can, then standards are as high as they can go. How can standards be higher than this? The only way to raise them beyond such a level would require reselecting the children who will attend school. Expecting children to do as well as they can, and reflecting this in the system of evaluating and reporting would seem to be a method of strengthening rather than weakening standards. It establishes a wholesome climate for achievement. It more adequately challenges the gifted as well as the slow. It is realistic as well as humane, and would seem to be in the best interests of all concerned.

Summary

The essential purpose of a system of evaluating and reporting progress is to provide information which may be useful in the continued development of the child. In something of a chronological sequence, elementary schools have tried the percentage method, the scale method, the modified-scale, the narrative report, and the planned-parent conference.

The search for quality in this discussion has attempted to rise above a more restricted issue such as competitive grading, and has identified *functions to be performed* by this aspect of the curriculum. Seven such essential functions have been described and interpreted. If one applies these functions to the older methods which tend to be favored by parents, he finds that *the older methods are incapable of adequately performing even a single one of the essential functions*. This is one of the interesting anomalies of the current scene. For people who sincerely seek excellence in their schools will, in this aspect of the curriculum, uncritically accept a reporting system which fails to report.

Excellence is reflected in schools which develop a system that can adequately perform the full scope of the task. A qualitative approach, therefore, is indicated by the degree to which the system:

1. Provides the kinds of information parents should know.
2. Describes and interprets a unique human being.
3. Makes provision for each child's evaluation of himself.
4. Communicates accurately what it seeks to convey.
5. Points up desirable forms of cooperative action.
6. Reflects the concept of fair play to all the children concerned.
7. Maintains the high standards of the school.

Chapter 12

Supportive Design

Curriculum design is the *superstructure* of curriculum organization. At its higher levels of quality or potentiality, it is a structure which is developed with great sensitivity to internal and environmental needs. It is thus an *external manifestation of internal conditions.* The primary defect of most curriculum design lies in the tendency to reverse this process. In such instances, design is arbitrarily frozen or imposed and teachers and children are required to fit into it as best they can. An imposed or frozen design is an error in conception. *Curriculum design should serve teachers and learners rather than rule them.* It must be able to bend and adjust to internal needs. It should continue to serve a role as an overall type of organization which rightfully exercises controls and gives a quality of cohesiveness to the total school organism; but it must be flexible enough to adjust to those continuing classroom needs which require and merit change. *The problem is one of combining order with flexibilty.*

The design of curriculum is regarded by many teachers as a remote consideration which does not relate itself in any important way to the teachers' work. Such an attitude is naïve. Curriculum design affects children and teachers in highly important ways. The design may be so vague as to cause teachers to feel insecure in the performance of their job. It may, on the other hand, be so restrictive as to prevent them from providing experiences that are needed by their children. It may, additionally, be so confused that excellent advances at one level are negated at another. Curriculum design is therefore an instrumentality which is intimately related to the quality of the learning environment.

This discussion of design has two central purposes. One is to orient the reader to selected background considerations that may be helpful in providing some degree of understanding and perspective with regard to the possible choices of curriculum design. The second is to pull from present understandings, some specific ideas which may be particularly desirable and necessary.

Designing Versus Design. Because curriculum design has often restricted teachers and children in a way that was detrimental to quality in the learning environment, some curriculum authorities in recent times have placed the idea of curriculum design in disrepute and have sought to replace it with the concept of designing. This would mean that a teacher would be relatively free from any preconceived curriculum plan, and that she could thus sit down with a group of learners and cooperatively develop a learning environment designed to meet their needs. There is, no doubt, a definite advantage to this concept, and a wise and skillful teacher might work with children in such a way that the curriculum could be close to their lives and be a genuinely worthwhile experience. The idea of an overall curriculum design, however, need not rule out the significant aspects of such an experience. It might instead actually provide for them. The broad aspects of an overall curriculum design operate as an orderly framework within which individual planning can better occur and also better relate to the efforts of others. Consequently, the cumulative effect of a six or eight year curriculum can be stronger. Care must be taken, however, not to make the planning too tight, else there is no opportunity to do the fine tuning and adjusting that is a professional necessity for each group.

Subject Designs. Carol was a very intelligent and enlightened first year teacher. She accepted a job with the Mars School District and was well pleased with her salary and the general level of wealth of the community. One day early in September she went in to her principal to clear arrangements for her children to visit the local museum. Her principal, Mr. Black, questioned her sharply about her reasons for visiting the museum and told her he thought she could use her time to much better advantage within the classroom. He reminded her that the content of the curriculum was heavy in fifth grade, and that the children would be doing well if they mastered all of their fifth grade texts. Carol thought Mr. Black was testing her. She pointed out that there were a number of items at the museum which were discussed in their unit on the early settlers, and that she knew her children would enjoy and profit from seeing them. She added that she thought there were many things that children could learn outside of books. Mr. Black suddenly became cool. He told her not to go to the museum and terminated the conference. Carol was shocked and returned to her classroom. She made an effort that year to fit into and adjust to a philosophy that was foreign to her own. At the end of the year she resigned and became an air line stewardess.

Mr. Black is an extreme conservative in his educational views. He is sometimes known as an essentialist. He tends to spend a great deal of time in his office. His files and records are apt to be very accurate and well-organized. He writes memoranda and bulletins to the teachers. He prides himself on being efficient. He keeps the machinery of his school well-oiled. He rarely gets into a classroom, and knows very few of the children in his school. The children and teachers address him carefully and respectfully as Mr. Black.

Mr. Black's concept of the learning environment reflects what has ordinarily been called the Subject Curriculum. His views on the curriculum are as follows:

1. A curriculum should be organized into parts called subjects. Thus, children study geography, history, arithmetic, etc.
2. The subjects should be arranged logically so that learnings at one level prepare the child for learnings at the next level. The content is largely preplanned by adults who best understand the subject matter.
3. The teacher's job is to cause children to master the subjects. The main focus should be upon the intellectual development of the child.
4. Methods of teaching are built largely around verbal activities. Questions, recitations, and lectures figure prominently in the teacher's direct contacts with children.
5. The teacher is the dominant and controlling figure in the classroom. He controls, directs, initiates, and brings to a close all classroom activities.

6. Books are the chief resource for learning. All children should have a copy of the same book.
7. Memorization is the major indication of achievement. Thinking is largely an adult activity. Children should learn and memorize the many fine things that adults have already thought and written in books.
8. Tests are the chief source of information as to what a child has achieved. The results are mysteriously grouped into amounts of achievement, and grades are assigned in accordance with the amounts.
9. Achievement is reported via report cards. Multiple types of achievement are jumbled together and reduced to symbols which are relatively meaningless. These symbols are then religiously conveyed to parents.

Mr. Black represents a potent force in the elementary schools. No one knows how many Mr. Blacks inhabit the schools, but Carol could easily have identified his educational beliefs before she signed her contract if she had visited and observed his school. There are many shades and varieties of Mr. Blacks, and some are more extreme than others. In general, they reflect what educators have called the book-centered school.

The proponents of Mr. Black's school like it because they believe:

1. That subject matter is basic and enduring.
2. Such a curriculum is easily organized and presented.
3. Most teachers and parents understand it and prefer it.

Opponents of the Subject Curriculum contend that:

1. The learnings are too compartmentalized and fragmentary. There are too many little appendages floating around with no apparent body or relationship to one another.
2. The curriculum is too far from the learner. Ignoring the interests and purposes of the learner results in great loss to the curriculum.
3. The logical arrangement of content is not necessarily logical to the child and therefore becomes a relatively useless bundle for learning and use.
4. Subject matter organization is not related sensibly or appropriately to the natural functions of every day living.
5. Subject curriculums do not develop habits of effective thinking,

inasmuch as they reflect a belief that the thinking has already been done and the job of the learner is to memorize it.

Activity Designs. Carol could have had a job with the Fairview District. Fairview had a reputation for being progressive in its school practices. Mr. White, principal of one of the older schools in the district, had taken her through the school in the spring when she was considering the position. Fairview was not a new building, but the rooms were attractive and colorful with their displays of childrens' work. She remembered that the children brightened perceptibly and seemed pleased when Mr. White came into their room. He seemed to know most of the children by name. He was relaxed and friendly with them, and showed a genuine interest in what they were doing.

Mr. White spent more than an hour with Carol that day, carefully showing her through the school. He asked her to observe as they went into different rooms to see if she could tell what unit or center of interest was in process. In almost each room she was able to do so, for the reading, language, and creative activity blended together to indicate a major emphasis. She was especially impressed with the childrens' creative efforts. Their art work was fresh and individualistic, and seemed to reflect a child's world rather than a world of adults. From the appearance of the rooms, she could see that the children pursued many different paths in their art work instead of making thirty-five identical looking tulips.

Mr. White showed her the school gardens and explained how he felt they contributed to the academic learnings. A bus pulled up and unloaded thirty-five flushed six year olds. Mr. White said that they had just returned from a trip to the zoo. Several mothers had accompanied them to assist the teacher with the trip.

It was a very pleasant morning for Carol. The teachers were friendly, the children were interested and responsive, and there was a wholesome atmosphere in the School. Carol would have preferred to teach at Fairview, but Mr. Black's district offered her $100 a year more salary.

Some people call Mr. White a Progressivist. He doesn't spend much time in his office and, unlike Mr. Black, there are times when he can't even find something in his files. He likes to know, however, what is going on in his classrooms. Mr. White believes that a school environment should be a relaxed and happy place where children can find many opportunities for development. His ideas stand in considerable contrast to those of Mr. Black. Mr. White's views of the curriculum may be summarized as follows:

1. A curriculum should be organized into centers of interest selected by children. Thus, children study the fireman, the circus, prehistoric animals, space travel, etc.
2. The centers of interest are arranged psychologically (logically from the point of view of the child). Pupil-purposing and planning today are the proper prerequisites for purposing and planning in the years to come. Information and skills will develop naturally in the process of pursuing one's genuine interests.
3. The teacher's job is to develop children along the broad lines of their present interests. The main focus is upon the total development of the child.
4. Problem-solving is the basic method. Teaching is largely a catalyst activity, functioning in such a manner as to develop in children the problem-solving approach.
5. The children are the dominant figures in the classroom. In growing measure they control, direct, and bring to a close their own learning experiences.
6. First-hand experiences are the chief resources for learning. Books are used as references. Each child in the classroom might logically have a different book.
7. Creative expression is the major indication of achievement. Memorization is imitative and relatively unimportant. If children can become creative, memorization is inconsequential and will largely take care of itself.
8. Observation is the chief evaluative technique and is directed toward evidences of personal growth and change.
9. Achievement is reported in personalized descriptions of the child as a unique individual. Evidences of growth, barriers to growth, and unique strengths and weaknesses are described. The report is generally conveyed by letter or personal conference.

Mr. White is also a potent force in the elementary schools. No one knows how many Mr. Whites inhabit the schools, but there are probably more Mr. Blacks today than Mr. Whites. There are many shades and varieties of Mr. White, and some are more extreme than others. Some, for instance, believe a child should study or undertake only those aspects of the curriculum which he wishes to study. Such advocates are rare, and most professional people who lean philosophically in the direction of activity design resemble the Mr. White that was described. In general, they reflect what may be called the child-centered school.

The proponents of Mr. White's school like it for the following reasons:

1. Children are more interested in what they are doing because the curriculum belongs to them and is close to them.
2. Greater interest inspires more effort and personal growth.
3. Development of the children is along more functional lines, such as purposing, thinking, planning, organizing, expediting, culminating, and evaluating.
4. Such a child development approach results in a better integrated, better developed child, more capable of taking his place in a shifting and dynamic society.

Opponents of the Activity Curriculum contend that:

1. Such a curriculum has little organization. The neat, expeditious form of subject organization is cast aside with no suitable substitute.
2. There is no continuity of experience. Children flit from a little of this to a little of that, leaving wide and important gaps in their learning.
3. Such a to-do about things of the here and now does not adequately prepare children for the future.
4. The curriculum lacks a conscious social direction.

Core Designs. Mr. Grey is principal of a school employing the Core Curriculum. Mr. Grey is a somewhat new type. Although he has elements of both Mr. Black and Mr. White in his philosophical orientation, he has a central emphasis which differs from them both. His motivation has a constant and deliberate social direction. Like Mr. White he has a keen interest in children but he is perhaps more of a sociologist. He does not believe that interests and purposes of children are the sole guides to learning experiences. He believes that they are important and he will try to identify and release them, but he will sift and channel them in such a way that they are directed specifically at the problems, the needs, and the aspirations of the culture. Whereas Mr. Black's school was book-centered and Mr. White's school was child-centered, Mr. Grey's school is life-centered. Mr. Grey sees the curriculum as deliberately reflecting and embodying the major elements of the culture. It is a synthetically created segment of life itself.

Mr. Grey encourages his teachers to use problem-solving as a basic method, but expects the problem-solving to be keyed to and directed at the real social problems that exist. He goes beyond this in his beliefs however. He sees the school as an instrument of leadership in social change. He would focus the curriculum on refining and improving the society itself. That is why he is often called a social reconstructionist. His school is not a passive and imitative organ like Mr. Black's, nor is it limited to using the community as a laboratory like Mr. White's. He aims to use the community as a laboratory for both discovery and improvement.

The compelling criterion for choices of learning centers or units of work in the pure type core is whether the problem is socially significant. A second criterion for the selection of units or problems is sometimes added in the form of a question. Can anything be done about the problem by the class if they do study it? If no possible solution or contribution seems possible with respect to this class, then the problem may be reserved for a group that can act upon it.

Core curriculums may emphasize such problems as safety, conservation, recreation, prejudice, and delinquency. Teachers in a core program should ordinarily be well trained in the social studies, for this area of the curriculum generally constitutes the core. Core theory generally reflects the following beliefs:

1. A curriculum should be organized around social problems or themes of social living. Thus, children study conservation, safety, production, inventions, etc.
2. The structure is fixed by broad social problems or themes of social living, such as making a living, governing ourselves, producing and distributing goods, etc.
3. The teacher's job is to help children understand, adjust to, and constructively refine and improve their corner of the world.

4. Problem-solving is the basic method, but the problems must be socially-oriented. Teaching is largely a catalyst activity functioning in such a manner as to develop in children the problem-solving approach.
5. Society and its needs and aspirations are the dominant consideration. Children and teachers work together cooperatively to help fulfill its needs.
6. Social problems from real life are the chief resources for learning. Books, pamphlets, films, etc., are supplementary. Life is the master text.
7. Improvement of the social problem or aspect of social living is the major indication of achievement. Purpose, attitudes, and effort are blended to achieve this end.
8. Observation is the chief evaluative technique, and is focused on children's constructive participation as members of a team.
9. Achievement is reported in personalized, descriptive statements of the child as a unique contributor to the group and his personal qualities as a socialized human being. Attitudes and performance with respect to qualities such as tolerance, suspended judgment, critical thinking, fair play, etc., may receive special attention.

Proponents of the Core Curriculum claim the following advantages:

1. The curriculum is more life-like.
2. Being more life-like, it contributes more directly and significantly to the society it is designed to serve.
3. Its orientation is such that it may actually contribute to the improvement of the society itself.

Criticisms of the Core Curriculum often include the following:

1. The school is a conservative institution which best serves a society by perpetuating its culture rather than by actively initiating change.
2. Teachers ordinarily are not sufficiently well-grounded in an understanding of their own culture to function effectively in this design.
3. The problem of organization and sequence in core design is difficult and has never been adequately resolved.

Selective Factors. Perhaps the chief value in discussing and interpreting theoretical patterns of organization lies in the sharpening of one's perceptions of total strengths and weaknesses. The awareness of plus and minus factors in each possible approach may make it possible for a school to develop a more sensitive blend. Regardless of what pattern of organization is developed by a school, however, certain elements need to find expression if the program is to achieve excellence. The remainder of this discussion, therefore, is devoted to pointing up those factors which should find fuller expression in the curriculum design of a qualitative school.

Articulation

The design of a curriculum, whatever its form, should represent an articulated overall plan. Such articulation causes the beneficial aspects of curriculum from grade to grade to be cumulative, and increases its total possible influence. Articulation is a multicolored cloth and can be the beneficiary of a number of curriculum practices. At the content level it can be furthered by a telescoped review of the preceding year's work prior to presenting the content for the present grade, and also, by a telescoped preview of the next year's work at the conclusion of the work of the present grade. At the principles level it can be furthered by faculty participation in the identification and enunciation of the principles that are to be stressed throughout the program.

Some schools request teachers to exchange rooms occasionally for certain periods so that a teacher who is to receive a group of children next year can gain more understanding of the group and a more intimate picture of their present program. The continuing-teacher plan in which a teacher goes on with her group to the next grade is also a practice contributing to the articulation of the program. Ordinarily, horizontal articulation is sought by forming curriculum committees composed of all the teachers of the same grade in order to cross-fertilize and coordinate their efforts. Additional articulation may be gained occasionally by vertical organization of the committees. Many additional practices can be used, but the basic point which is involved is that a design, in order to be qualitative, must reflect features which contribute to the articulation of its parts.

Eclectic Form

The overall plan of a curriculum should be an eclectic or hybrid form. It cannot be a pure Subject Curriculum, nor a pure Activity Curriculum, nor a pure Core Curriculum. From a theoretical point of view it is desirable and helpful for curriculum authorities to identify and interpret the pure types, but from an operational point of view it is rarely feasible for a school to emulate them. There are several reasons for this. One such reason is that an attempt to implement a pure-type curriculum tends to put one's thinking in a bind. *The direction of the curriculum may be influenced more by the question of what is desirable to do in order to implement this design, than what is desirable to do in order to improve this learning environment.* A second significant reason is that the points of view of individual members of a faculty are so diverse that it is practically impossible to get solid faculty-community approval of any of the pure types, and without this solid approval no design can be successful regardless of its intrinsic merits. The design which is used, therefore, will have to represent those particular elements of the common designs which can gain major faculty-community approval. An eclectic design is the only one which can achieve such a degree of acceptance.

The reader should recognize the controversial element in this proposal. Purists will contend that the mixing of philosophies and designs produces a weakened philosophy or design. The history of hybrid forms refutes this. The blending of strengths creates a stronger product. Even, however, if some weakening in the design should occur in the eclectic form that is derived, there is a dividend from the presence of vigorous faculty-community support which should more than compensate for the loss.

Priority Content

The eclectic design should have some elements of content pinned down for special emphasis and mastery. The designation of *priority content* suggests that it is very selectively derived, in the sense that it is believed to be important for most children to know. Most children in our society should, for instance, develop number and language skills in order to adjust intelligently to their environments. An excellent curriculum would include elements of content which have been carefully evaluated and identified as especially valuable in a given school. It would not be necessary for priority content in one school to be identical to the priority content of another school. Common elements of content, however, would be more apt to exist in this segment of the curriculum inasmuch as the intent is to point up common learnings that are important to the development of children in general.

Such content should be selected by representatives of the parties involved, and should be chosen by a rational process involving the deliberate use of criteria of content slection. It is envisioned that the content emerging from such a process would be less in amount than what currently exists in most schools, due to the high degree of selectivity employed. Three advantages might accrue from such a quantitative reduction of amount. One advantage is that the content which remains has a better chance of being learned, for it has received special recognition and will receive special emphasis. A second advantage is related to articulation. The streamlined curriculum for each grade reduces the size of the total overall plan to the point where it is more comprehensible to the entire faculty. More importantly, however, the content reduction makes room for other vital elements of overall curriculum design which should become a part of an eclectic approach.

Optional Areas of Study

The time saved by reducing the required content should be specifically reserved for optional areas of study of a functional and enrichment nature in each grade. These areas should be cooperatively developed by the professional personnel of the school. They should be high in interest value, and should represent varying levels of difficulty. Such areas should be characterized by a high degree of permissiveness or freedom with respect to what children and their teachers do with them and about them. The purpose of this is to build flexibility into the design. The curriculum design should explicitly state the desirability of this time being planned and used cooperatively with the children. The margin of time for this aspect of the curriculum should itself be flexible and should be governed in large part by the interest of the teacher in using curriculum time in this freer fashion, and her skill in using it effectively. It is entirely possible that two teachers of the same grade in the same school might differ widely in this respect. One of them might be spending 90 percent of her time on a subject approach to the required content, and might be using only 10 percent of her time on the cooperative, optional aspects. Yet, for her that 10 percent approach is a new experience and a forward step. She is trying her wings. Perhaps next year she may use 20 percent of her time in that manner. Another teacher may comfortably and effectively use as much as half of her time on a freer, more interrelated type of approach. Each teacher is entitled to try to do her job as she sincerely feels she can do it best. Little good can come from arbitrarily imposing on either of them restrictions that are personably unacceptable to them.

Pupil-Teacher Planning

Within the optional areas of study there must be a deliberate attempt on the part of the faculty to grow in its ability to *plan with* children in identifying areas of study and individual interests which are of importance to the children themselves. The act of planning is a growth experience vitally needed in a democratic society, and this element of quality is not typically a feature of subject design. Too frequently, the Subject Curriculum may reflect a belief that planning is a function to be exercised more exclusively by the mature. It thus ignores the process by which one becomes mature. Children cannot learn to plan without planning any more than they can learn to swim without swimming. Presumably, one becomes more mature by having opportunities to participate with growing skill and intelligence in the functions of maturity. The act of planning is such a function. It is a real-life skill which is just as important as learning one's multiplication tables, and perhaps much more so. Furthermore, such an aspect of a child's personal development has a much higher transfer value to his daily living than much of the subject matter content he will be required to learn.

There is no intent to imply here that pupil-teacher planning is an act which should take place only in the optional areas of the curriculum. The suggestion is that such planning must occur at least within these areas. The curriculum would be qualitatively improved in an approach which weaves elements of effective democratic planning throughout many aspects of the school day. Such planning brings the curriculum closer to children. It helps them feel that they are an important part of the school enterprise, and it develops positive desires on the part of children to make their school program a success. The planning concept is a process concept. It is an idea which is an essential part of the philosophy of the Activity Curriculum. It is an idea which may be identified with Core philosophy only if the planning has deliberate social direction. In the manner in which it is presented here the idea does not connote deliberate social direction except in the sense of the value skill in planning has to a democratic culture. It is not intended to limit the planning of areas of study and interests to those which have a deliberate social direction. Such a limitation would needlessly restrict the curriculum. Obviously, the curriculum should possess deliberate social direction, just as a nourishing diet should include protein. The elimination of all foods except protein, however, would result in a less nourishing diet, just as the elimination of all curriculum which was not socially-oriented would result in a qualitative loss to the learning environment.

Problem-Solving

Within the curriculum there should be obligation as well as opportunity for children to select and attempt to solve problems which are of genuine concern to them. Perhaps it is overpretentious to dignify this activity by the term problem-solving; however, it does embrace the essential elements of problem-solving. It seeks to develop in children a greater power to (1) identify a problem, (2) collect data concerning a problem, (3) formulate hypotheses or possible courses of action, (4) test the hypotheses, and (5) evaluate the results. The Subject design is weak in this respect, for it reflects a belief that the task of the young is to learn what others have thought rather than to learn to think. Problem-solving is another process-concept. It brings into the curriculum a powerful element of quality which is identified as the basic method of both the Activity and the Core design. Like genuine pupil-teacher planning, it adds strength to the curriculum in the sense of emphasizing children's purposes and understandings, and it has exceedingly high transfer value as a real-life skill. Again, there is no intention here to imply that problem-solving should have outlet only in the optional areas of study. Problem-solving can be the basic approach to science in the curriculum, and it is a basic and important aspect of the social studies as well. The point is that problem-solving in some form and to some degree is an essential aspect of a qualitative design. Furthermore, the problems which are included in the curriculum should represent two types: (1) those which are important to children whether or not they have deliberate social direction, and (2) those which have some significant social direction, whether or not they are of primary concern to children. Problems of living obviously do not confront people merely on the basis of self-choice.

Planned Deviation

In the further interest of flexibility, the occasional need for deviation from even the required elements of content for any given grade should be recognized, and the conditions for deviation should be stated. Failure to reflect this idea in the curriculum design will, in all probability, result in a lack of adjustment to important group needs. The group may be ready for something more challenging and advanced than what is prescribed for them, or they may not yet be advanced to the point where they can successfully undertake it. Unless curriculum design is explicit with respect to deviation in this sense the children will be given content irrespective of its value to them, for many teachers are hesitant to make major adjustments out of fear of criticism from the teacher who will receive the children next year. The most important basis for such adjustments should be the professional judgment of the teacher that the deveiation is necessary in terms of what is best for her group. The curriculum design should clearly indicate that it is not a teacher's professional privilege, but her *professional obligation to make whatever curriculum adaptations are necessary to facilitate the well-being and success of her group.* Such deviations should be a matter of open policy, and should be communicated to all parties that are interested and affected by the curriculum change.

Planned Curriculum Review

The design of curriculum should be reviewed by all the elementary teachers at least once a year. This review or evaluation might be appropriately held in the spring, while the experiences of the past year are still fresh. The basic question involved in this review is how the curriculum might be improved from the point of view of the children and teachers of each grade. Children should participate in this annual review on a very permissive basis with their teachers in each room prior to the adult discussions. The stage should be set for the planned review in such a way as to permit very free and candid discussion of the issues involved. The discussion should be chaired by an elected member of the group rather than by one of the status leaders of the school. Ideas feeding from the curriculum committees would come before the total faculty in such a discussion, but ideas from the floor should receive equal consideration.

Action Programs

Ideas and recommendations from the planned curriculum review should be acted upon. The annual review cannot be a dynamic factor in the appraisal and improvement of curriculum design unless its ideas bear fruit. Nothing destroys the vitality and general level of morale in curriculum improvement more than the practice of actively soliciting ideas which are later politiely ignored.

Acting upon an idea does not necessarily require its adoption throughout the entire system. Many ideas can be given a trial run in some portion of the total system in order to check on their merits. Such a trial run should be conducted by those who are primarily interested in its success, and should be launched in a setting conducive to its success. A change in reporting to parents, for example, from letter grades to planned parent conference might be tried out as a pilot study in the school having the most interest in making such a change. It might also be initially limited to the parents of the first graders, inasmuch as those parents are likely to be the younger parents in the community and the most responsive to a newer approach.

Action programs are indicative of a healthy learning environment and reveal the presence of a growth edge. Good ideas must be tried or they tend to lose their strength. The thoughtful testing of ideas, with a consequent sharing of the results, is one of the most fruitful and stable paths to an improved curriculum design.

Summary

The design of a curriculum is the overall plan or type of organization. It gives a quality of cohesion to the total program, but it must achieve this cohesion in a manner which allows teachers and learners to function without senseless restrictions. Variation within the program should in fact be regarded as an obligation rather than a privilege.

Pure-type designs rarely occur in a given school due to complications arising from the differences in point of view and circumstances that impinge upon the school. Thus, the program must ordinarily be a blend, but the quality of the blend stands to be improved if the strengths and weaknesses of each of the pure types is understood.

Design is supportive when it is sensitively created in such a way that the factors associated with excellence in the classroom can find expression and encouragement in the overall organization. Nine factors which are supportive in this sense have been interpreted in the discussion. Thus, the design of a curriculum in the qualitative school is one which:

1. Uses an eclectic form.
2. Achieves an articulation of the parts.
3. Establishes a priority content.
4. Stimulates optional areas of study.
5. Encourages *real* planning *with* children.
6. Provides genuine experiences in problem-solving.
7. Creates the conditions for essential deviations.
8. Maintains a dynamic curriculum review.
9. Responds adequately to the continuing need for change.

Chapter 13

Reflections

The preceding chapters have presented an image of the qualitative elementary school. The image is comprised of eighty-three ideas which have been selected as factors associated with an excellent program. Each of the factors is believed to be important in influencing how much and how well children learn, as well as what they are to become.

Many factors associated with excellence have been omitted, for the presentation has attempted to be illustrative rather than comprehensive. It has attempted to capture the spirit if not the complete substance of a qualitative school. In spite of omissions, however, the nucleus of eighty-three factors is believed to be a very powerful array of ideas. In their totality they reflect an impressive concentration of excellence in the program.

Desirable though they may be, each of the ideas should be subjected to thoughtful evaluation in the classroom. Such evaluation leads to a refinement and improvement of the ideas themselves. Many ideas about good programs may be expendable, but the dedication to excellence is not. Thus, factors such as those that have been proposed may serve as a point of departure in the appraisal of the present program of a school. Appraisal of this nature raises the level of understanding of the strengths and weaknesses of a program, and leads not only to improvement of the program but to improvement of the criteria of appraisal as well. This is the kind of creative implementation which characterizes an excellent school.

As in the case of any given era, the present is interesting, and in a sense tragic as well. For more than fifty years professional education has nurtured in the schools practices which could make the child's early years a happier and more significant experience. These ideas have slowly taken root, and many of them have only recently become implemented on a wide enough front to be truly effective. Now the gains stand to be erased by shrill voices which are all too frequently uninformed about the deeper consequences of their acts. Perhaps the mechanism of reaction always tends to regress beyond the point that reason itself would dictate. Human intelligence can control reaction, however, so that what is swept away is the weaker elements of the structure rather than the strengths. This is one of the significant acts of leadership which must be displayed in to-day's school.

Such leadership does not imply that a school should ignore the voices of its constituents. The voices should be qualitatively weighed; they should not, however, be permitted to exert an influence that is disproportionate to their worth. Thus, the push-button executive who urges a return to the McGuffey readers should be heard, and should receive the response which his superficial recommendation deserves. In the same vein those who attack all efforts of the school to improve its mental hygiene also have a right to be heard. It would be well to hear them, however, in the presence of a specialist whose experience with the psychological problems of children has provided abundant evidence of the need for schools to improve their facilities for professional guidance and care. If adequate representation occurs for responsible as well as irresponsible views, mass erosion of the gains of half a century of educational thought will be less likely to happen. Selective retention of strengths continues to be one of the basic conditions for success.

Although the schools must continue to support a kind, humane, and protected environment they should strive for intellectual excellence as well. For the nature of the world is such that the first-grade child in America cannot continue to count popsicle sticks if his Soviet counterpart is to learn geometry. Our schools must compete with their monolithic adversary, but they must at all costs rise to the challenge of achieving excellence and supremacy in the image of the American eagle instead of the Russian bear. An eagle requires a different curriculum than a bear. If he makes the mistake of imitation he becomes inadequate as an eagle and even less adequate as a bear. Imitation is the surest road to tragedy.

The eighty-three factors are one answer to the challenge that Russia has thrown at our schools. They are culled from the traditional framework of the school so that they may be more easily understood; they are traditional, however, only in the finest sense of the word. They seek to capture some of the best of the past and present practices of the school, but they look also over the horizon to tomorrow and try to build additionally for what is yet to come. The spirit that is manifest throughout the ideas is the spirit of excellence, but this spirit never abandons the concept of respect for human personality and justice to all concerned. The presentation tries to give to the curriculum a quality of gentleness along with its muscle, and a quality of the heart as well as the mind. If the ideas are thoughtfully and creatively implemented they will help to transform the learning environment into a qualitative school.

Appendix

Summary of Qualitative Factors

The qualitative elementary school has been interpreted as one which:

GENERAL
FACTORS

1. Engages in some form of major goal-directed activity.
2. Uses a multiple-offense approach.
3. Produces demonstrable results.
4. Reaffirms its concern for the well-being of each child.
5. Reflects an unmistakable love for our way of life.
6. Demonstrates a flexible and enlightened administration.

SOCIAL
STUDIES

7. Uses the classroom and environs as a laboratory for social living.
8. Stresses its unique opportunities for developing ideals.
9. Highlights a selective core of information.
10. Cultivates critical thinking.
11. Provides gradative experiences in self-direction.
12. Strives for additional depth in its program.
13. Consciously balances its content and methods.
14. Applies the concept of quality control.

SCIENCE

15. Accepts scientific thinking as its major goal.
16. Emphasizes process over content.
17. Provides for functional extension of learnings.
18. Attempts to select science-oriented teachers.
19. Contributes positively to personality development.
20. Teaches the science of health.
21. Teaches the science of safety.
22. Directs its evaluation to the major goal of scientific thinking.

LANGUAGE
USAGE

23. Establishes an enlightened setting.
24. Sets realistic goals.
25. Identifies its priority content.
26. Organizes a cooperative analysis and attack.
27. Develops a love of language.
28. Places a special emphasis upon vocabulary development.

LANGUAGE
TOOLS

29. Gives a priority to the core vocabulary of spelling.
30. Uses spelling's booster mechanism.
31. Adds a systematic enrichment content.
32. Weaves in its individualization material.
33. Capitalizes on its secret weapon.
34. Organizes the program by levels.
35. Teaches phonetic generalizations.
36. Evaluates mastery in context.
37. Maintains manuscript throughout the program.
38. Keeps its personal obligation to children.

TEACHING
READING

39. Utilizes and builds upon the experiences children have had before they come to school.
40. Concentrates on procedures for maximizing the incidence of success during the first year.
41. Provides for the strengthening of meager backgrounds by resources that are built into the program itself.
42. Stresses sufficient phonetic elements to achieve the earliest possible achievement of independent reading.
43. Strives for maturity of word perception through the emphasis of multiple approaches to word attack.
44. Relates any given approach humanely and effectively to the capacities of the children involved.

MATHEMATICS

45. Continues to stress meaning and self-discovery in its approach.
46. Develops and uses conceptual aids as an intrinsic part of the meaning approach.
47. Provides for systematic use of functional arithmetic.
48. Makes *judicious* use of diagnosis.
49. Emphasizes problem-solving over mere computation.
50. Provides an accelerated program for those who should accelerate.
51. Tempers "the beefing up process" by filtering fun throughout the total program.

CREATIVITY
52. Utilizes the total creative thrust of the curriculum.
53. Works actively to heighten the senses themselves.
54. Provides special opportunities for children to think of things "as they are not."
55. Cultivates a sensitivity and responsibility for beauty in living.
56. Encourages and increases the incidence of creative teaching.

DISCIPLINE
57. Retains an enlightened permissiveness at home and at school.
58. Strives for a healthy form of self-control.
59. Operates sensitively within the proper limits of adult authority.
60. Adjusts its practices creatively to the circumstances and the child.
61. Moves deliberately forward in the substitution of understanding for rules.

GROUPING
62. Uses maturity as a factor in admission, in addition to mere chronological age.
63. Implements a nongraded form of school organization at least in the primary grades.
64. Builds diversity with a controlled vertical range deliberately into the composition of each class.
65. Balances any ability groupings to be used with the recognized antidote of success.
66. Forms additional groupings specifically designed for the personality needs of children.
67. Bases the regrouping of children on patterns of growth instead of the school calendar.

EVALUATING AND REPORTING PROGRESS
68. Provides the kinds of information parents should know.
69. Describes and interprets a unique human being.
70. Makes provision for each child's evaluation of himself.
71. Communicates accurately what it seeks to convey.
72. Points up desirable forms of cooperative action.
73. Reflects the concept of fair play to all the children concerned.
74. Maintains the high standards of the school.

SUPPORTIVE DESIGN
75. Uses an eclectic form.
76. Achieves an articulation of the parts.
77. Establishes a priority content.

78. Stimulates optional areas of study.
79. Encourages real planning with children.
80. Provides genuine experiences in problem-solving.
81. Creates the conditions for essential deviations.
82. Maintains a dynamic curriculum review.
83. Responds adequately to the continuing need for change.

Index